Therapeutic Trampolining for Children and Young People With Special Educational Needs

T0383550

This practical resource explores the benefits of therapeutic trampolining on children and young people with special educational needs. It supports practitioners as they introduce the trampoline into their own therapeutic settings.

Trampolining is known to improve balance, co-ordination and motor skills; it can improve bone density and benefit the lymphatic and cardiovascular systems. It has even shown to encourage communication in children with autism and PMLD.

This book draws on the author's extensive experience of delivering both the British Gymnastics Trampoline Proficiency Award scheme as well as the Rebound Therapy trampolining programme. The book also explores the practical side on how to set up and deliver trampolining as a therapy in schools, clubs or in the home.

Photocopiable material includes:

- Lesson equipment, such as schemes of work, lesson plans adapted for varying needs and a trampoline rules poster.
- Tools for offering therapeutic trampolining sessions such as sequencing cards, communication cards, Risk Assessment, an individual education plan and a communication placemat.
- All the necessary forms to ensure a safe trampolining environment for all participants, including screening forms, referral and assessment forms and relevant policies.
- A business plan for after school provision, advertising leaflet and service level agreement.

This is an invaluable resource for anybody looking to explore therapeutic trampolining as a way of enhancing the physical and emotional wellbeing of children and young people with special educational needs.

Ange Anderson, M.Ed. is a SEND consultant and additional inspector for special schools specialising in therapeutic and technological interventions for additional learning needs. She is the former headteacher of a leading specialist school and author of special educational books and children's books. She has authored several educational articles and papers on therapeutic intervention, is involved in international research work and has presented internationally on topics related to special education.

@Angelique500 on Twitter
Email: Angelique5@hotmail.co.uk

Therapeutic Trampolining for Children and Young People With Special Educational Needs

A Practical Guide to Supporting Emotional and Physical Wellbeing

Ange Anderson

Routledge
Taylor & Francis Group

LONDON AND NEW YORK

First published 2020
by Routledge
2 Park Square, Milton Park, Abingdon, Oxon OX14 4RN

and by Routledge
52 Vanderbilt Avenue, New York, NY 10017

Routledge is an imprint of the Taylor & Francis Group, an informa business

British Library Cataloguing-in-Publication Data
A catalogue record for this book is available from the British Library

Library of Congress Cataloging-in-Publication Data
Names: Anderson, Ange, author.
Title: Therapeutic trampolining for children and young people with special
    educational needs : a practical guide to supporting emotional and
    physical wellbeing / Ange Anderson.
Description: Abingdon, Oxon ; New York, NY : Routledge, 2020. | Includes
    bibliographical references and index.
Identifiers: LCCN 2019050365 (print) | LCCN 2019050366 (ebook) |
    ISBN 9780367819293 (hardback) | ISBN 9780367819286 (paperback) |
    ISBN 9781003010869 (ebook)
Subjects: LCSH: Physical education for children with disabilities. |
    Trampolining—Theraputic use. | Trampolining—Physiological aspects.
Classification: LCC GV445 .A64 2020 (print) | LCC GV445 (ebook) |
    DDC 613.7/042087—dc23
LC record available at https://lccn.loc.gov/2019050365
LC ebook record available at https://lccn.loc.gov/2019050366

ISBN: 978-0-367-81929-3 (hbk)
ISBN: 978-0-367-81928-6 (pbk)
ISBN: 978-1-003-01086-9 (ebk)

Typeset in Optima
by Apex CoVantage, LLC

Visit the companion website: www.routledge.com/cw/speechmark

Dedication

This book is dedicated to all of those striving to get trampolining recognised as a Paralympic sport.

Contents

Contents

Figures

Figures

Tables and downloadable resources

Preface

Global educational reform is thankfully taking hold and countries have been rethinking how they engage students in education. Before students can be engaged in education, they need to be in the right frame of mind to learn. This is particularly so for those students with Special Educational Needs (SEN). It is time that all schools looked at how to provide emotional and physical wellbeing through therapeutic interventions so that their students can return to the class ready to engage.

Trampolining is one of the most exhilarating, exciting and joyful of sports. Going on a trampoline for children can be likened to children going on a bike. They don't think of it as exercise but as having fun. A bike will take you from A to B, but a trampoline will let you soar! Over the years I have used the trampoline with many students that have either learning difficulties, or physical disabilities, or both. Barring days when students were unwell every student has felt that their turn on the trampoline ended too soon. They returned to class in a better frame of mind than when they left it, and the exhilaration they found from trampolining travelled with them.

So, what magic does the trampoline hold that no other vehicle for learning does? How can we use the feel-good factor it gives to encourage cross-curricular teaching? Can it show benefits for the physical and emotional health and wellbeing of students with learning difficulties? How does it specifically help students with Autism (ASD), Attention Deficit Hyperactive Disorder (ADHD), Dyslexia, Dyspraxia and those with Profound and Multiple Learning Difficulties (PMLD)? Is trampolining for those with learning difficulties just available in schools or outside of school too? Do you need to be trained and who provides suitable training? Can students with learning difficulties enter competitions, and if so to what level?

What kind of trampoline should you get if you want one in your garden or even in the home? What good are mini trampolines? How can you support a person with special educational needs who attends your trampoline club or trampoline park? How can you set up your own club? This book aims to answer these questions and more.

How to use this book

The chapter titles will guide you. If you wish, for example, to understand autism and how to support students with autism in the classroom, during a physiotherapy session or at a trampoline club or trampoline park through trampolining, there is a full chapter on the subject. You may find ideas in the different chapters that you wish to adapt for students with other learning differences.

I have included trampoline schemes of work for those with ALN and for those with PMLD, six-week lesson plans, consent forms, screening forms, contraindications form, risk assessments, a trampoline rules poster, trampoline record sheets, evaluation forms to show impact on learning, communication board, trampoline sequence cards, a business plan, policies and more that you may photocopy and use.

I have used trampolining to enhance the physical and emotional wellbeing of students for many years. I have found that it has the knock-on effect of putting students in the right frame of mind to learn and that it can create moments of magic for the progression of communication.

Acknowledgements

I would like to thank Eddy Anderson, founder of Rebound Therapy; Colin Robson, founder of Preston City Trampoline Club; Heather Sargent, founder of Twisters, Cardiff; Ross Whittaker, director of Northampton Trampoline Gymnastics Association and Fiona Reid, Chief Executive Officer for Disability Sport Wales, for giving up precious hours to meet, talk to me and correspond with me about their work and what they have done to further the sport of trampolining for those with learning disabilities.

I would also like to thank all of the staff at the different special schools, trampoline clubs and parks that I was allowed to visit that appear in this book.

I would particularly like to thank Donna Roberts, headteacher of Ysgol Hafod Lon in Penrhyndeudraeth, and Rhona O'Neil, headteacher of Ysgol Tir Morfa for allowing me so much extra time in their schools observing trampoline sessions. And of course I would like to thank Sue Price and Julie Cousins, both lead Rebound therapists at Ysgol Pen Coch and Kathleen Glendenning, Senior physiotherapist for the NHS, who cared as much as I did about providing trampoline therapy, and found the funding for the trampoline at Ysgol Pen Coch when the school opened.

Abbreviations and glossary of words and phrases used in the book

The following words and phrases will usually appear in the text in full on the first occasion they are used. Subsequently the abbreviation is used.

AAC	Augmentative and Alternative Communication
ADD	Attention Deficit Disorder
ADHD	Attention Deficit Hyperactive Disorder
A&E	Accident and Emergency part of a hospital
ALN	Additional Learning Needs
AoLE	Areas of Learning and Education
ASD	Autistic Spectrum Disorder
BG	British Gymnastics
Big Mak	low-tech communication aid that you can record on
BSGA	British Schools Gymnastics Association
CeDR	Centre for Disability Research
DBS	Disclosure Barring Service
DCD	Developmental Coordination Disorder
DIR	Developmental Individual Relationship
DMT	Double Mini-Trampoline
DOB	Date of Birth
DSNI	Disability Sport Northern Ireland
DSW	Disability Sport Wales
EFDS	English Federation of Disability Sport, now known as Activity Alliance
FEDLS	Functional Development Emotional Level
GMPD	Gymnastics for People with Disabilities
GP	General Practitioner (doctor based in the community)
IATP	International Association of Trampoline Parks
ICT	Information and Communication Technology
IEP	Individual Education Plan
INAS-FID	International Sports Federation for Athletes with Intellectual Disabilities
IQ	Intelligence Quotient

LED	Light Emitting Diode
MBE	Member of the Order of the British Empire
MKT	Musico-Kinetic Therapy
NASA	National Aeronautics and Space Administration
NDP	National Development Plan (competition pathway for trampolining)
NGB	National Governing Body
NTGA	Northampton Trampoline Gymnastics Academy
NHS	National Health Service
PCTC	Preston City Trampoline Club
PEC	Picture Exchange Communication
PMLD	Profound and Multiple Learning Difficulties
PNS	Parasympathetic Nervous System
PSHE	Personal, Social and Health Education
PTA	Parent Teacher Association
RDA	Riding for the Disabled Association
REM	Rapid Eye Movement
RfL	Routes for Learning
RoSPA	Royal Society for the Prevention of Accidents
SaLT	Speech and Language Therapy
SDS	Scottish Disability Sport
SLD	Severe Learning Difficulties
SNS	Sympathetic Nervous System
TEACCH®	Treatment and Education of Autistic and related Communication Handicapped Children
TPD	Trampolining for People with Disabilities
TUM	Tumbling
UN	United Nations
UK	United Kingdom
UV	Ultra Violet light
VIP	Venture Into Play

Bed – part of trampoline used to bounce on
Dismount – the way a person moves from the trampoline bed to ground level
Hands and Knees Bouncing – trampolinist goes from feet onto hands and knees
Mount – the way a person moves from the ground level onto the trampoline bed
Spotters – people stationed around the trampoline to support a falling or tripping trampolinist

Trampolining – supporting emotional and physical wellbeing

If you can jump on a trampoline and bounce, then when you jump in the air for a split second you feel as though you can fly, the weightlessness is uplifting, and you can't help but smile. When a student with profound and multiple learning difficulties is hoisted onto the trampoline and gently bounced, they smile. Light bouncing can help increase blood flow to underused muscles and it helps the body release endorphins in the brain (which make us feel good and so we may smile). Large trampolines and mini trampolines are an amazing resource that all schools can benefit from if you want to support your students' emotional and physical wellbeing.

In 2019 nearly 40% of London's youngsters were reported as overweight or obese (Jarvis 2019) and trampolining was suggested as a way of encouraging fitness and emotional wellbeing through fun. Anyone who has taught students with autism and any parent of a child with autism knows that not much encouragement is needed when a trampoline is available to support that child's emotional and physical wellbeing.

In 2016, the UK government published guidance on obesity and weight management for people with learning difficulties stating that 'It has been recognised for many years that people with learning disabilities are at an increased risk of being overweight compared to the general population, with poorly balanced diets and very low levels of physical activity. This risk, in turn, increases the likelihood of a range of health and social problems'(2016). The guidance detailed the issues faced by them and their families and recommended diet and exercise. There is a limit to the exercises available to a person with PMLD. Trampolining is one of them.

George Nissen invented and built the modern trampoline in 1936. NASA began to use those trampolines soon after. NASA recognised that astronauts returning from space were losing 20% of their bone density on return to earth and had to find an exercise that would increase bone density quickly. When the astronauts were tested on a rebounder compared to the treadmill, there was less pressure on their joints due to the G force. When rebounding and on top of the bounce, your G force is eliminated, meaning you are weightless for a split second and when at the bottom of the bounce, the G force is doubled providing an adequate stress on every cell in the body to promote change. Some physiotherapists began to see it as a useful piece of equipment. It is worth noting that the use of trampolines for some medical conditions is not recommended and, in every case, consent forms and medical forms must be completed and signed before any student takes part in a trampoline session. Templates of consent and contraindication documents can be found in chapter 7.

A study was undertaken for NASA by Bhattacharya et al. (1980) comparing running, jogging, walking and bouncing on a trampoline. The results showed that jumping on a trampoline was less stressful to the neck, back and ankle than jogging on a treadmill for an equivalent oxygen uptake. In fact, the study concluded that 'any activity on a rebound unit is more efficient than a treadmill running at any speed' (Bhattacharya et al. 1980, p. 887).

It can easily be observed in a special school that a student with injuries or a painful disability finds it less painful to exercise in the hydrotherapy pool or on the trampoline than they do on solid ground. NASA reports suggested that there was no undue stress on the body from being on the trampoline and that there was less output and less demand on the heart compared to other exercises. The oxygen consumption with the trampoline was almost twice as efficient as running.

NASA reports suggest that bouncing on a trampoline increases cellular excretion of toxins and protects against cellular degeneration, which makes it a great exercise for students with degenerative diseases.

It improves lymphatic flow. (The lymphatic system does not have a pump like the heart and so is reliant on the body to move to push things through the lymphatic system.)

According to NASA's research, it has less impact on the joints than running on concrete as the impact is absorbed by the springs. It enhances immunity to ward off infections. It helps with digestion because the rhythmic up-down motion of bouncing stimulates the contraction and relaxation of muscles that make up the digestive tract. It helps improve balance, coordination and posture by stimulating the ocular nerves and inner ear canal. It increases lung capacity and oxygen intake; bouncing on the trampoline has been proven to increase metabolic rate. All these things support the emotional and physical wellbeing of students with special educational needs who can be affected by any one of these conditions or a combination of them.

Subjects who had acquired new motor skills due to trampolining showed a statistically significant increase in rapid eye movement (REM)-sleep according to researchers in Germany (Buchegger 1991; Erlacher et al. 2016). REM sleep aids learning and problem solving.

Trampolines provide us with the opportunity to follow physiotherapy programmes in a more play-centred approach. I have found that students sometimes dread having physiotherapy done to them but do not dread going on the trampoline and in fact look forward to it.

The first time your student gets on a full-sized trampoline, encourage them, if they are able, to move around it – it has different tensions in different places. The most stable, bouncy part is the middle and this is where we position students who are unable to move for themselves. Sample schemes of work and lesson plans can be found in chapter 7.

Special schools can use a trampoline to follow physiotherapy programmes with any of their students. They can devise their own sensory programmes, or they can adapt the British Gymnastics Proficiency Award scheme (see section 1 of the Appendix) to meet the needs of students. I have used the trampoline to deliver cross-curricular subjects of literacy, numeracy and PSHE to students with various types of learning differences. They can also have staff trained in Rebound Therapy. There is a cost involved but sometimes funding is available.

Sensory trampoline sessions

Sensory sessions on the trampoline can be tailored to meet students' sensory needs. Sensory trampoline sessions are an extension of the curriculum already supplied and the teacher does not require any trampoline qualifications to deliver these sessions but does need to feel confident using the trampoline. An understanding of health and safety and trampoline rules (found in chapter 9) would aid this confidence.

Students may be hyposensitive or hypersensitive to sensory stimulation. If the student is hyposensitive, they will need additional sensory input to feel content. If they are hypersensitive, they may see, hear, smell, feel things that the ordinary person doesn't notice. A sensory trampoline session will take these into account and a session should be an extremely pleasurable experience for that student. The session should see a decrease in tension and a decrease in behavioural issues due to sensory needs not being met. Some ideas for a sensory trampoline session follow.

- If a student enjoys music and has a preference, then the session can include that. Staff tend to keep a supply of preferred music available and will only play it if the student shows that they are enjoying it as some students are hypersensitive to particular frequencies. I recall one student who loved electronic music. No one else in that class did, and they would get upset if they heard it. He enjoyed his trampoline sessions even more because he would have his electronic music playing in the background as he was bounced lightly and followed his physiotherapy programme on the trampoline. (Physiotherapy programmes are devised by qualified physiotherapists who show class staff what to do. This is not usually done on the trampoline, but they follow this up with visits to ensure the programme is being delivered properly and give guidance when requested.) Sometimes more physiotherapy can be done whilst the student is relaxing as they often do not realise that they are doing more exercise than they would ordinarily.
- Some students find noise frightening and want a session that is completely quiet. Staff gauge how much pressure to put on the bounce of the trampoline so that the experience is pleasurable. It might just be that the coach holds the student from behind so that they can feel any tension in the student's body as a slight bounce is initiated. The session might just consist of gentle bounces and no physiotherapy will take place. In my 29 years of using the trampoline with students, I have never come across a student who didn't enjoy trampolining. I may have been lucky.
- If a student enjoys the feel of materials on them, then parachute games can take place on the trampoline. Parachute games are used frequently in special schools outside on the playground but there is nothing that can prevent it being used on the trampoline, except the staffing of it. This tends to need at least two adults who can inflate the parachute and be at either ends of the trampoline. It is better, though, if a couple of spotters are also available so that each corner of the trampoline is covered by the parachute for maximum effect. The student is gently bounced as the trampoline inflates and deflates above them. They are cocooned within the trampoline. Rainbow parachutes can be purchased from many educational suppliers. We bought ours from www.tts-group.co.uk
- Some students really enjoy the feel of bubble wrap when on the trampoline, and staff have been known to save large sheets that come with furniture delivered to their homes and bring

it into school for use on the trampoline. You can also purchase rolls of it if you wish. Some students like the feel of netting/satin/velvet/fake fur, and these can be placed on the trampoline to encourage students to move towards them so that they get some vestibular and proprioception input as well as the sensory stimulation of touch. This technique works equally well for those who enjoy auditory stimulation and will move towards a familiar squeaky toy.

- Some students enjoy bubbles being blown as they sit on the trampoline and move around it trying to catch the bubbles. (Care is needed here, and the trampoline needs to be covered in material that can be washed afterwards.)
- Some students are thrilled by a trampoline filled with balloons that welcomes them as they enter the room. Their task may be to push all the balloons off the trampoline, meaning that they will also be using their vestibular and proprioception senses as they move about the trampoline. If the student has a fear of the balloons bursting, then different-sized balls can be used. I remember doing this for the first time for a 14-year-old student with PMLD in 1999. She was not interacting. I knew she liked balls and wanted to try anything that would encourage her to interact. When she entered the trampoline room and saw all the balls, some large physio balls, footballs, play balls of all sizes and loads of ball-pool balls, her face lit up. She managed to push all the balls off the trampoline twice. She was so excited and stimulated by the session that she vocalised all the way to the shop, which was her next session, and continued to do so throughout the day. It was a turning point in her communication that I cherish to this day.
- Some trampoline rooms have interactive overhead screens so that students can lie back, relax to their favourite music as they look up at the overhead screen. These interactive screens can encourage the student to move on the trampoline to make the images on the screen change.
- Some students love to have smelly objects to reach for or a favourite smell sprayed in the room. This needs careful managing and should be the last session of the day so that the room can be aired ready for the next day as not all students like smells and some are hypersensitive to smell.

Mini trampolines

In 2002 David Beckham's physiotherapist, Alan Smith, used a mini trampoline as a therapeutic aid so that David could continue to practice whilst recovering from a foot injury (Winter 2002). The rest, as they say, is history. Since 2002 mini trampolines have become increasingly popular in schools.

Mini trampolines have been used in sensory circuits in both mainstream and special schools for many years. They are used in both the Alerting phase and the Organising phase (see chapter 6 for more information on sensory circuits). Sensory circuits support students with sensory processing disorder.

Mini trampolines do not take up as much space as a full-sized gymnastics trampoline and so many schools are increasingly using them to deliver therapeutic intervention to aid anxiety and hyperactivity in students. Some of these schools have them in classes and students can take themselves off to calm down before returning to their work task. Other schools buy in sessions on mini trampolines delivered by outside agencies to develop wellbeing (see chapter 6 for more information).

Reboundtherapy.org and World Jumping UK have recently teamed up to work on a mini trampoline therapy called Flexi-bounce so that students can continue rebound therapy activities at home and during the holidays without the need for a full-sized trampoline. It can also be used in the classroom in addition to rebound therapy sessions on the full-sized trampoline if necessary. Go to www.worldjumping.co.uk to find out more.

Rebound Therapy

The term 'Rebound Therapy' was coined by the founder of ReboundTherapy.org, Eddy Anderson, also known affectionately as the Godfather of Rebound Therapy, to describe the use of trampolines in providing therapeutic programmes for people with a wide range of special needs. The programmes are available from their website and from Winstrada, the national body for the promotion and development of recreational and therapeutic gymnastics and trampolining (www. winstrada.com). I spoke with Eddy recently. Eddy reports that the early work was in 1972 and progress was slow because then it was by word of mouth.

Today Eddy is still working with schools and with young people with special needs delivering to about half a dozen workshops each year. He still gets an enormous amount of pleasure from the responses from staff and users. Eddy gives credit for ReboundTherapy.org progress as a leader in the field of trampoline therapy in large measure from the work done by colleague Paul Kaye with the advent of the internet and their collaboration for the past 12 years.

Eddy would tell you that his background was unusual. He did three years in the Parachute Regiment, followed by seven years in the Royal Air Force as a Physical Training Instructor. Due to a knee injury, he then moved to civilian life as a Remedial Gymnast and qualified at Pinderfield's Hospital. He worked with special needs children in the then Junior Training Centre (no schools for those most in need in those days).

He trained as a teacher and spent two years in mainstream primary and then became a Deputy Head at Horsforth special school in Leeds. Five years later he was appointed Head at Springwell School and was able with a supportive team in Hartlepool to put in place his passion for movement as a central mode for real communication. In 1992, Eddy, with support from Cleveland lea, produced a validated 'train the trainers' course for special schools with co-tutor Lynn Schofield. He retired from teaching at 56 and set up his Rebound Therapy consultancy (having won the best invention of the year 1993 for his water-based trampoline, the Original Floatation).

In 2006, Eddy joined forces with pioneer disability sports coaches and founders of the Saturn V association of gymnastics and trampolining clubs, Paul and Shirley Kaye. They formed the ReboundTherapy.org website and consultancy.

In 2008, Eddy and his team piloted a national train the trainers training course to enable schools and centres to produce a complete protocol for the training, implementation and development of rebound therapy sessions specific to the needs of their school or centre. Very timely for me, as in 2009, I opened a brand-new special school in North Wales. I had been trained in Rebound Therapy while at a previous school and valued its benefits. Before the school opened, I ensured that I had a staff member trained as a train the trainer in Rebound Therapy and negotiated with the lead physiotherapist in the area for a full-sized trampoline to be donated to the school.

In 2014 Ysgol Pen Coch began delivering a yearly conference on therapeutic interventions for special education. We were very lucky in 2016 to have Eddy Anderson introduce the 2016

Figure 1.1 Delivering Rebound Therapy at the 2016 conference

conference. He then delivered Rebound Therapy to very willing participants throughout the day. What a great and humble man!

In addition to following physiotherapy programmes on the trampoline, some of the students followed the Winstrada Development scheme for students performing at level 1, which is a Rebound Therapy level. At Ysgol Pen Coch only students with PMLD, who are hoisted onto the trampoline, used the trampoline. The trampoline in use at that school is a regular sporting trampoline. Unfortunately, with a ceiling height of only 6 feet it made it unsafe for ambulant students who may be able to perform at level 2 and above. Rebound Therapy is levels 1–3 of the Winstrada scheme, but students with PMLD at Pen Coch have remained at level 1 throughout their time at school.

Since 2016, the Sir Stanley Matthews Foundation has been involved with Rebound Therapy. I observed Rebound Therapy staff at Tir Morfa special school in Rhyl who had been trained through that charity. That charity is now taking on the project of training the trainers for Rebound. On completion of the Therapy Course, the trainers will become Sir Stanley Matthews Rebound Therapy Coaches and will be expected to represent the Foundation with values that were part of his life.

Rebound Therapy is becoming a popular trampoline therapy in other countries too. The IATP (International Association of Trampoline Parks) is recommending the Rebound Therapy training course for its members.

The Rebound Therapy Association for Chartered Physiotherapists (RTACP) promotes Rebound Therapy and has produced guidelines on Rebound Therapy and suggests that it can:

- Raise low tone or lower increased tone
- Increase body part awareness, spatial awareness, proprioception and sensory awareness

- Promote relaxation
- Challenge balance to help improve dynamic balance issues
- Increase vocalisation in those with reduced vocal ability, creating a gateway to communication, sometimes giving squeals of delight
- Gasps and intakes of breath can also stimulate the cough reflex

As with any physiotherapy intervention, there are contraindications that need to be considered before any treatment can occur. Please see chapter 7 for contraindications.

Musico-kinetic Therapy

Musico-kinetic Therapy (MKT) is a therapy that uses the trampoline and live music performance. Using sound therapies is not new. We have used Vibro-acoustic Therapy successfully at Pen Coch for several years and have also employed a therapist in music on the staff ever since the school opened in 2009.

Musico-kinetic Therapy is different in that it combines both live music and exercise. On the face of it, it appears to be a wise thing to do. We know music therapy can have a calming effect on students. We know ourselves the calming effect music has on us as individuals. We know that trampolining is an enjoyable form of exercise. To put the two together could be genius.

Most special schools will use music in the background for trampolining with some students. YouTube even has a selection of music specifically for use during trampolining. I have seen music used often for students with profound and multiple learning difficulties (PMLD) who can find concentrating on trampoline exercises too strenuous. Having music on in the background can be relaxing and combined with the gentle bounce of a trampoline can be very therapeutic and may be all that is required for an emotionally relaxing session.

The research done into Musico-kinetic Therapy has been done with people with traumatic brain injury (Kato 2004) and those in a vegetative state (Noda et al. 2004). The research findings were that Musico-kinetic Therapy may be therapeutically effective in facilitating the recovery of brain function following therapeutic hypothermia. The results of the other research were consistent with the hypothesis that MKT is useful for improving the emotional condition of patients in a persistent vegetative state, especially those with severe brain damage caused by trauma.

This fits with my observations of the effect of music and trampolining on students with PMLD. It would be interesting to see if live music had an even greater effect on those students. It would be an interesting piece of comparative research.

If you wish to see Musico-kinetic Therapy in practice go to: www.youtube.com/watch?v= m9tE3WWdyyQ (brief intro to musico-kinetic therapy 2018).

2 | Trampolining for students with profound and multiple learning difficulties (PMLD)

What is PMLD and how can we support those with PMLD?

The words 'profound and multiple learning difficulties' suggest that the student has more than one disability and that one of these is profound. Often these disabilities include sensory and physical impairments. They could be blind or deaf or both. They could have dysphagia, which is a disorder of swallowing that can lead to aspiration problems. Sometimes they will have a particularly rare syndrome. Sometimes the condition is degenerative. They can also have autism, attention deficit hyperactive disorder, dyspraxia, dyslexia and other learning difficulties that become secondary to their primary diagnosis. Some are life-long wheelchair users. Their communication is usually non-verbal and they often use the same communication skills that most people used as babies: Eye gaze, facial expressions, copying, body posture, gesturing with head, arms and hands, physically reaching out to things, positioning themselves either too close to or away from situations they wish or don't wish to engage in, vocalisation, touch and other tactility to name but some. Often, they have little intentional communication and rely on self-advocacy for their needs and wants to be interpreted. The vulnerability that is so much a part of their lives reveals our own limitations. How do we know what they want or need? This means that the student has an enormous number of disadvantages to overcome in order to learn. On the positive side, at least nowadays it is expected that students with PMLD attend school. Some attend trampoline clubs.

Maureen Oswin (1931–2001) was a writer and researcher on the care of children with severe learning disabilities. Her books, *The Empty Hours* (1971) and *Children Living in Long Stay Hospitals* (1978), highlighted the poor treatment of these children in the institutions that they were expected to stay in. She documented how people deteriorated so that they became more and more immobile which led to associated health problems including scoliosis. She informs us that it was thought by those in control of these institutions at the time that the condition that the person was born with would ultimately lead to deterioration and that there was no point in trying to reverse it. Margaret Oswin's books helped fuel the drive to move children out of hospitals and ultimately to the closure of the institutions. It is hard for me to accept that this was less than 50 years ago.

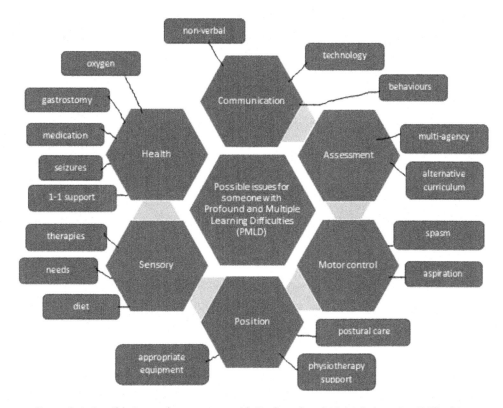

Figure 2.1 Possible issues for someone with Profound and Multiple Learning Difficulties

Postural care and positioning are a vital part of a student's day at school. Handling and positioning guidance from occupational therapists and physiotherapists working with the educational team can enhance the performance of students with multiple disabilities (Rainforth & York-Barr 1996). Any physical activities done with students with PMLD must be done with the support and the guidance of these therapists.

Staff in a class that has students with PMLD will be tasked with more than just supporting education. They will be involved with dressing and undressing, toileting, changing pads and washing students. They will also be required to give those regular positional changes as well as massage and stretching as directed by the physiotherapy team. They will be expected to assist with eating and drinking as directed by the speech and language therapists.

In my experience students with PMLD are more likely to have epileptic seizures and staff need to be prepared to undergo training to deal with these occasions in a calm manner. Many of the students that I have taught have needed a gastrostomy and staff are required to be trained in this precise procedure. Sometimes they will be asked to deliver oxygen and undergo necessary training. To be a member of staff who works with students with PMLD can appear daunting, but in all honesty the pleasure of working with such amazing resilient people outweighs the demands of the job. I speak from experience as I was a teacher in charge of classes for PMLD students for several years in different schools and a member of the senior management team in these schools. I was also headteacher of a school where our students with PMLD were integrated into other classes. I am constantly reminded that they desire to communicate, to make their needs and feelings known and to be respected.

It is my opinion that communication is the biggest challenge for students with PMLD. Students with PMLD are often non-verbal and communication difficulties can lead to frustration and

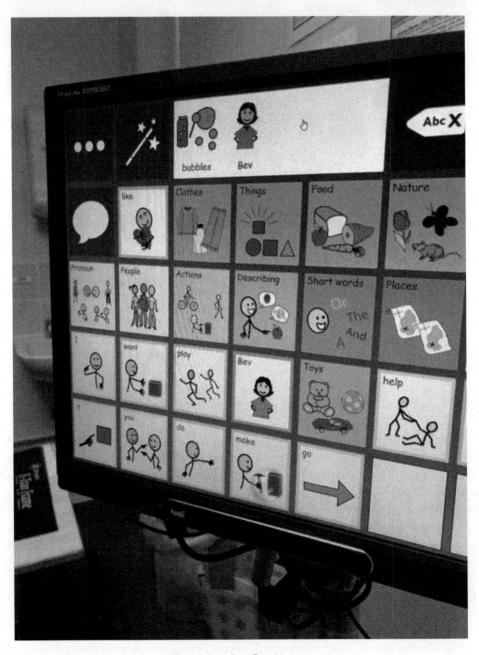

Figure 2.2 Eye Gaze in use

behavioural issues. Intensive interaction has been used in all the schools I have led. To find out more, go to www.intensiveinteraction.co.uk/about/how.php.

Total communication, including the use of signing, is the approach that most special schools use today. The Total Communication Policy is outlined in section 2 of the Appendix.

Technology, in particular, the Eye Gaze, has helped students with PMLD to communicate effectively. As headteacher of a special school I am very familiar with the use of Eye Gaze technology and its success. Eye Gaze machines are high-tech devices that require the precise movement of the eye to search for the word or picture required and the device will speak the visually selected word. With the EyeMobile Plus, users who are able, can navigate their Windows tablet, control and access Apps, internet, social media, games, the Microsoft Office suite and more giving users greater personal freedom and levels of independence. One of our students was unable to communicate by other methods and was labelled as PMLD until he used the Eye Gaze. He was able to show everyone just what he was capable of and is now using the tablet version.

Technology continues to evolve and the future potential for meaningful communication is huge.

Continuous assessment of students with PMLD and the opportunity for an alternative curriculum that meets their needs is essential. Many students with PMLD benefit from a more therapeutic curriculum that supports their sensory needs, postural care, health, motor control and communication.

Trampolining

I have yet to see high tech successfully used for communication during trampolining, but I am always thrilled by the advances of technology and look forward to the possibility. In my most recent experience therapists have relied on low-tech battery-operated buttons, Big Maks, communication books and PECs. Sometimes the student will respond by the nod or shake of the head, vocalisation, gesture or sign that they want more etc. In my experience all students take their means of communication with them to use during the trampoline therapy sessions and students have been observed transferring skills learned and developed during their trampoline session back to the classroom. This has been documented as evidence that trampolining impacts on the student's learning.

Therapists I have worked with themselves note that communication is the area where the most rapid development occurs during therapeutic trampolining purely because the student must communicate if they want 'more'. Therapists tell me that there is a myriad of ways that students communicate this and some examples encountered by the therapists are a tap on the trampoline itself, a touch on the therapist's arm, use of the Makaton sign for more, direct eye contact and vocalisations.

Therapists report that trampolining motivates students, that they become excited when they see the therapist enter the class, perhaps anticipating a trampoline session. Therapists report that the students listen to instructions more because the therapists will not continue with the session until they get a response from the student that they want the session to continue.

There is nothing to prevent a student with PMLD from accessing a trampoline club as long as they have trained support with them. I have attended clubs in 2019 where students with PMLD are welcomed.

Figure 2.3 Low-tech buttons and Big Mak communication aids

A suitable curriculum

'Learned helplessness' is a term often used for students with PMLD because things are done for or to these students and these then become habits. It is similar I guess to how we now treat those diagnosed with severe dementia. Technological breakthroughs could change this.

Governments all over the world are looking to change school curriculums to meet the individual needs of students. For the first time the Welsh government has allowed a curriculum that meets the needs of individual students. As headteacher of one of the pioneer schools for the Welsh government, I have been involved in introducing the new curriculum to schools in Wales as well as the training of staff to deliver the new curriculum.

A curriculum for those with PMLD must meet their needs. They, as all students if we are honest, need to be in the right frame of mind before they can learn. Students with PMLD face the ordinary issues every student faces daily where they may get up and not feel like going to school, mum and dad may have had a row and they could be feeling anxious, breakfast was a bit rushed etc. On top of that they could have had a sleep-deprived night due to their illness. They could have had an epileptic seizure. They could be severely constipated. Their condition could be degenerative. In my experience they will still go to school. It is important therefore to notice changes in their behaviour, mood or general demeanour. It is important that the curriculum is flexible enough to meet their needs.

It is worth bearing in mind that students with PMLD in the UK have historically only received an education by attending school for the last 50 years. Compare that to the first act of Parliament for education being passed in 1877 where it was compulsory for ordinary children to attend school from the age of 6 until the age of 16 years. The curriculum for the ordinary student constantly evolves but the ordinary curriculum does not meet the needs of those with PMLD. I have found that a therapeutic curriculum meets the needs of students with PMLD.

It is important to remember that education is not about preparing a nation for the workforce; it is about preparing a nation for life itself. The life of a person with PMLD is as important as the life of a person without any disabilities. It is just different. That means that education is all pervasive and happens even when a student is being changed. How do we change them? Are we rushing the changing process so that we get in the queue for Rebound Therapy quicker? Or are we taking our time and noticing that they lifted their leg for us to put their shorts on? The very fact that someone does not talk does not mean that they do not try to communicate but how we respond does make a difference in whether they continue to try or whether they give up and give in to learned helplessness.

Education for someone with PMLD is not just academic. It is about helping them to learn self-care skills, mealtime skills and how to best recover from a seizure or spasm with support. It is about posture support and going into a standing frame or a walking hoist and why it is important. It is about receiving physiotherapy. It is about taking medication, and if necessary, oxygen and learning how to swallow so that aspirations are less likely to occur. It is about learning how to adapt to a gastrostomy and a restricted diet. It is about doing all these things whilst also having sensory needs. If a student is deaf, how are you going to explain these important life skills to them? Are you just going to do it to them?

In order to know what to teach students with PMLD, you must help them with all the previously mentioned items and find out where they excel and what they are interested in. This knowledge usually comes from the parents. This knowledge will help determine an individual educational plan for the student. An individual behaviour plan may also be needed.

I recall a beautiful young girl I taught several years ago when I was in charge of a class specifically for those with PMLD in a secondary special school. She was 12 years old and had Niemann Pick disease type C (see Section 3 in the Appendix for more information). Her older sister had died of the disease when she was 15. The doctors initially did not think Alison had the disease that her sister had. Alison attended an ordinary primary school and was running around like any child at 9 years of age. She began having seizures and lost her fine motor skills at 10 years of age. She joined our special school, where her sister was, when she was 11.

Her condition deteriorated rapidly. She lost her speech and was wheelchair-bound by the time she was 12 and I joined the school. Her sister had recently died of the disease, and it appeared that Alison was going through depression. She had apparently previously had such a sunny disposition.

What kind of curriculum do you give to a student like Alison? It is no good assuming that all students with PMLD have the cognitive age of a two-year-old and therefore need to have stories that you would read to a two-year-old. Being a teacher in an ordinary mainstream school is hard enough but ensuring that you meet the needs of someone like Alison as well as nine other students, each with a similar, yet different story, can be difficult. There is no majority of ability to aim your lesson towards. Every student requires an individual lesson plan as well as their individual health needs being met.

Alison was a typical teenager. She loved Boyzone and in particular, Stephen Gately. One of her favourite parts of the curriculum was Rebound Therapy on the trampoline. She had the freedom of being out of her wheelchair. As she took part in Rebound Therapy, Stephen Gately and Boyzone would be singing in the background on a CD player. She was enjoying being bounced while lying on her back. She was able to let staff know if she wanted more bounces and if the music stopped, she would soon demand that it was put back on. She would wait patiently for her turn on the trampoline and seemed to enjoy both the lead up to her session as well as the session itself.

Rebound Therapy

Rebound Therapy is a form of exercise and an area of the curriculum that even students with the most profound sensory and/or physical impairments enjoy. It is a form of trampolining that can be tailored to suit any need. A good majority of students with PMLD are wheelchair-bound and therefore could be confined to wheelchairs for most of the school day. Relevant therapies provide a rich context within which to develop fundamental skills and understanding. I have seen students who spend a lot of time in a wheelchair and standing frame become excited and cheerful when they know that they are going to have a trampoline session.

Often the sessions follow the Winstrada Grade 1 of the trampolining programme compiled in association with 'ReboundTherapy.org' – which is the official UK body and international consultancy for Rebound Therapy. Grades 1, 2 and 3 are based on the Rebound Therapy coach/teacher training course. These can be adapted to meet the needs of students and often additional aids are used that are recommended by physiotherapists. Rebound Therapy is used to facilitate movement, promote balance and promote and increase muscle tone, improve fitness and improve communication skills.

Therapeutic aids and the trampoline

In the picture you can see Nessie® in use for a student with PMLD at our school. Made from flexible, low-density foam, Nessie® is light enough to be portable but heavy enough to offer positioning support during trampoline therapy. The bumps and contours of Nessie® have been shaped to provide support during the primary positions associated with physical play therapy.

This photo shows the student long sitting. This is an important part of child development, encouraging head control, hands to midline and reaching for toys. Nessie's unique 'bumps' encourage transverse weight bearing through arms and shoulders.

In the next picture you can see Nessie® being used by our trampoline therapist for tummy time, which supports physical development by strengthening neck, shoulders, arms and back, and is an important foundation for the transition to sitting via side lying/side sitting. This is a position supported by all child development workers, e.g. health visitors and physiotherapists. Nessie® can also be used in the home without the use of a trampoline. The trampoline just makes it more fun to use. Students who use Nessie® in schools would associate it with a pleasurable experience and be more inclined to accept its use in the home. (See www.specialisedorthoticservices.co.uk/product/nessie/ for more information about Nessie®.)

Another useful piece of trampoline equipment for those at the early stages of trampolining is something known in special schools as the Peanut.

The Peanut Roll was born from joining two balls together and creating a tool which allows for a great use variety and a higher stability as against the ball. It has been used in the physiotherapy sector for many years, and it is ideal for those who have coordination and balance difficulties.

Figure 2.4 Long sitting on Nessie®

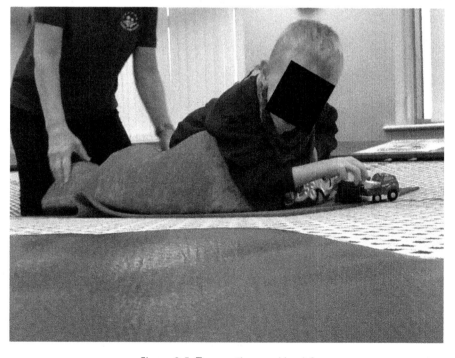

Figure 2.5 Tummy time on Nessie®

Figure 2.6 Balancing on the Peanut Roll

The Peanut is latex-free and offers greater stability than regular, round therapy balls by limiting movement to forward and backward. The unique design allows a therapist and a student to sit together on the Physio Roll. Students can also sit in the centre cradle for maximum comfort and support. One of our students, who is wheelchair-bound, is doing just that in the photo.

Students with PMLD have limited access to exercise. In some schools it is limited to physiotherapy sessions where often a teaching assistant follows a programme devised by a visiting physiotherapist. The exercise routines of schools that I have worked in have been enhanced using the hydrotherapy pool and the trampoline. In both situations a physiotherapist can be asked to devise the programmes to be followed. Children who ride bikes don't see it as exercising. In the same way children who follow physiotherapy programmes on a trampoline don't see it as exercising. Yet it has been noticed in schools that I have worked in that a person coming to take a student with PMLD to the trampoline gets a welcome smile but a physiotherapist coming to do an assessment gets a frown.

Please see chapter 7 for a trampoline scheme of work for students with PMLD that you can copy and use.

3 Trampolining for students with autism (ASD)

What is autism?

I have worked with young children, teenagers and adults with autism for many years and they are all very different. Just the same as ordinary people are each individual and different from each other.

Since 1998 (Blume 1998) the term 'neurodiversity' has been used to describe those whose brains work differently to the neurologically typical brain. Their brains are different in their function and anatomy. Judy Singer, an Australian sociologist, first used the term 'neurodiversity' in her sociology honours thesis in 1998 to describe those with autism. She added that it was a group name for diverse clusters of behaviours that had in common impairments of 'Social Communication'.

These differences can affect their ability to communicate and to socialise. It can affect their ability to control their behaviour and to manage their anxieties. It can also affect their ability to control their movement. Martha Leary and David Hill (1996) liken the differences to those suffering with Parkinson's disease, Tourette syndrome and Catatonia. In other words, this is not a choice the child makes, these traits are quite outside their control due to their central nervous system disorder.

Sensory information processing

Most of the students with autism that I have worked with have had sensory information processing difficulties. Sensory information processing difficulties are when we over-respond because we are hypersensitive, or under-respond because we are hyposensitive, to the sensory information that our bodies constantly receive through the receptors that we have all over our bodies. Hearing is the most common sensitivity and students can easily be distracted by noises that the ordinary person can filter out. I recall attending a talk given by an adult with autism who told us she could hear the radiators and the light fittings working in the classroom and those noises prevented her from concentrating on what the teacher was saying. She told us that a visit to the seaside was torture as the noise of the waves was deafening to her. Touch is another common sensitivity that I have found affects a lot of the students with autism that I have encountered. Their parents have

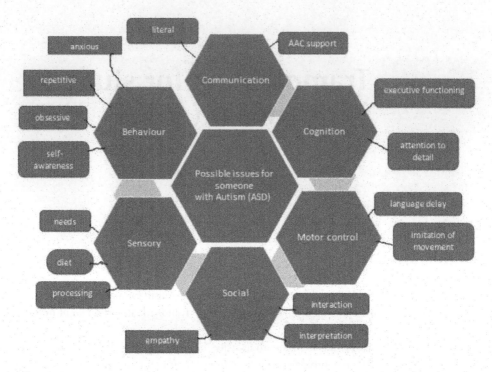

Figure 3.1 Possible issues for someone with Autism (ASD)

had to watch what products they use to wash the clothes and they must remove labels. There is currently no known cure for sensory disorders but through education, understanding and in some cases medication, the effects of the sensory disorders can be minimised.

Often the diets of students with autism are affected because of their sensory needs. In my experience most students with autism that I have worked with have preferred to eat dry foods. Bread, dry toast, bread sticks, rice cakes, crisps (usually a variety that a student feels tunes in to their taste buds) have been staple favourites at lunch and snack times. Very few of the students with autism that I have worked with have eaten school dinners. Those that have prefer the airline trays to dinner plates as the different foods can be separated from each other more easily. Sometimes a student with autism may feel nauseous in the school canteen. Lunchtime in schools could be volatile if catering staff are not on board and if schools do not take account of dietary and sensory needs. Thankfully, as a society, we are becoming more tolerant of dietary quirks.

Cognitive functioning

Executive functioning are the processes that help us regulate, control and manage our thoughts and actions. Anyone who has worked with students with autism knows that they struggle with this. Sometimes this struggle can lead to a meltdown (see section 4 of the Appendix) and sometimes stimming (see Section 7 of the Appendix) is their way of coping when they feel out of control.

Attention to detail is an asset that allows students with high performing autism or Asperger's syndrome to excel in music, art, maths, science and more. Students can be highly skilled in areas that interest them. Stephen Wiltshire MBE is known to be able to look at a subject once and then draw an accurate and detailed picture of it.

Motor control

Sensory processing disorders can lead to problems with motor skills. In addition, MelloMontiero and his colleagues found that 'numerous histopathological and magnetic resonance imaging studies have reported reduced volume in the fastigial nuclei and cerebellar vermis lobules VI-VII in children with ASD. This is a region supporting ocular motor function, verbal working memory, and speech coordination' (2017). This could be a reason for language delay.

When we refer to language development in autism we often mean in relation to cognitive and social skills. The development of motor skills can support language acquisition skills and needs to be considered (Bedford et al. 2015).

Communication

Every school should have a Total Communication Policy. You can find one to adapt in section 2 of the Appendix. I have found that those with Asperger's and high performing autism show by their reactions that they can take other people's words as literal. They often don't understand idioms or flippancy.

Instead of saying 'Are you happy to take this test?', a teacher or indeed a doctor would get a better response by asking 'Are you willing to take this test?'

Instead of saying 'I'll be with you in just a second/just a minute', you would save a lot of angst by saying 'I'll be with you in a moment'. A moment is not measurable. It is highly likely that those on the spectrum, who also have severe or profound learning difficulties, have these additional problems.

Augmentative and alternative communication (AAC) is an umbrella term for communication methods used to add to or replace speech or writing for those with impairments. It should support them in the understanding of the spoken or written language. It should support them in their own spoken or written language.

AAC includes simple systems such as pictures, gestures and pointing sometimes referred to as low tech, as well as more complex techniques involving technology and referred to as high tech.

I have found picture exchange cards (PECs) particularly popular for students with autism. The student will give you a picture card in exchange for the item on the card. I have seen the use of PECs lead to the acquisition of speech but there is no empirical evidence for this. Nevertheless, it is still a useful tool for communication and has worked particularly well in my experience at snack times.

Students with autism who can read would use word cards instead of picture cards and in some instances, words can be written out there and then as a request or response. With the advancement of technology PECs can now be used on iPads, saving staff huge amounts of time making

Figure 3.2 PECs booklet

Figure 3.3 Using an iPad App

cards. The PECs Phase III App, designed to look just like a PECs communication book, is an invaluable tool for teaching picture discrimination.

Sign language is something we all use at times instead of speech. We wave goodbye. We nod hello. We sometimes wink to let people know we agree with them. Other examples of low-tech communication are body language, gestures, pointing, eye pointing, facial expressions and vocalisation.

Aided communication usually involves technology of some kind. This can be as simple as a button or a Big Mak that speaks once pressed. iPad Apps and small portable tablets can provide students with a host of familiar words that once pressed speaks for them.

Twenty years ago, if your child was non-verbal, your resources were very limited. Advanced communication was limited to low technology. Nowadays the iPad has revolutionised the assistive communication world. At an affordable price, the easy-to-use iPad has become the most recommended device when an assistive communication device is needed. In the iPad App store, there are numerous applications available for individuals with autism. They vary in price and new ones are being added regularly.

Social

As ordinary humans we constantly use facial expressions and body language without thinking and these add subtle nuances to whatever we are saying. In my experience students with autism who can speak are more direct with no nuances and cannot easily interpret facial expressions or body language. A lot of work is done in schools to help students with autism read facial expressions. There are a lot of good Apps, added to daily, that are available to support this.

Behaviour

Many of us are familiar with a student with autism's need to rewind. When DVDs and video tapes were popular, I noticed how several students rewound to a specific part that they needed to watch time and time again. It was both repetitive and obsessive. Yet the underlying reason could have been anxiety. Students with autism are anxious a lot of the time. The autonomic nervous system is classically divided into two subsystems – the sympathetic nervous system and the parasympathetic nervous system. The sympathetic nervous system puts the body into fight or flight mode, and I know many colleagues who would say students with autism are in this constant state of sympathetic arousal because they are always under stress and fearful of the real world. The parasympathetic system promotes digestion and counterbalances the sympathetic functions enabling a person to become calm and function appropriately. It is possible that trampolining can activate the parasympathetic nervous system to decrease anxiety.

It must be very hard if you have autism trying to make sense of a world that bombards you with information all the time and seems to constantly invade your personal space. I have also noticed through studying many behaviour reports as well as observing students with autism that their behaviour escalates if a perceived wrong is not dealt with immediately. This can lead to a meltdown (see section 4 of the Appendix). As we come to understand the condition more, we can make allowances for students' different perspectives and find ways for them to channel their anxieties before a meltdown occurs. A few minutes on the trampoline can work for some students.

Most of the students with autism that I have worked with require routine, rules, timetables and benefit from TEACCH® stations (see section 5 of the Appendix). Trampolining requires routine. There are some who can't cope in a structured environment and I have found that a DIR® Floortime™ approach (see section 6 of the Appendix) works better for them. It is a play-based approach to learning that is child- rather than teacher-led. Students tend to regard trampolining more as play than work and so trampolining appears to be a win/win activity. It is useful to bear in mind that working with students with autism should not be a power struggle. If the adult sees it as a power struggle, it can lead to confrontation and a waste of that adult's energy. It could be more effective to have a mini trampoline available in the classroom or nearby so that the student can have some time out to de-escalate. There is the additional benefit of not having to fill in a behaviour incident form too.

Trampoline benefits and considerations for students with autism

The following are benefits and considerations of trampolining for students with autism.

- Trampolining is not a team sport so students with autism can excel at this sport.
- Students with autism can benefit from using a full-sized trampoline and can also benefit from using a mini trampoline. Mini trampolines are now commonly used as part of a sensory circuit for students with sensory processing disorder in both mainstream and special schools. Please see chapter 7 for lesson ideas for both the full-sized trampoline and the mini trampoline.
- Trampolining is a sport that relies on sequences, routines, rules and timetables. It is ideally suited to students with autism who rely on sequences, routines, rules and timetables.
- Transition can be difficult for students with autism. Ensure the transitions to and from trampolining are planned and supported transitions.
- The physical sensation and movement of jumping up and down can help the brain process and organise incoming sensory information and help students with autism to interpret these signals.
- Students who are hypersensitive (over-sensitive) focus on detail. Bright lights can distort their vision. It is important the check out the lighting in the room where you provide trampolining.
- Students who are hyposensitive (under-sensitive) have a high pain threshold and could break a bone without feeling it by being over-zealous on the trampoline.
- Students with autism may enjoy weighted blankets on top of them and all schools that have students with autism should have weighted blankets. These can be used on the large trampoline and be part of a therapeutic trampoline session where a student is rolled up tightly in a blanket and the trampoline is bounced very gently.
- Students who are hypersensitive (over-sensitive) sometimes do not like to be touched, so this needs to be borne in mind by trampoline coaches and assistants.
- Students who are hyposensitive (under-sensitive) to sound love being surrounded by noise and so a noisy trampoline club would be no problem. Students who are hypersensitive to sound find that noises are magnified and sometimes distorted and would prefer a quiet trampolining session.
- Students who are hypersensitive to sound can hear background noises and so would need a trampoline coach to speak directly to them in a loud and clear manner. Students who are hyposensitive to sound do not hear sounds clearly and so would also need a trampoline coach to speak face to face in a loud and clear manner, perhaps accompanying the directions with signs, if possible.
- Students who are hyposensitive (under-sensitive) in proprioception have no awareness of where their body is in time or space and so they can easily fall over on the trampoline and

could find it difficult to stand unsupported on the trampoline. An assistant or coach would need to support them on the trampoline until the student clearly shows that this is no longer necessary.

- Students who are hypersensitive (over-sensitive) in proprioception tend to need to move their whole bodies to look at something. When a coach or trampoline assistant wishes to demonstrate or show this student something, then they need to allow time for the student to change position in order to do so.

- On the other hand, studies show that when learning from errors that were sensed through proprioception, it was found that children with ASD outperformed typically developing children. Yet they underperformed typically developing children when learning from errors that were sensed through vision (Crocetti et al. 2015). This suggests that the trampoline could be a good cross-curricular learning forum for students with ASD.

- Students who are hyposensitive (under-sensitive) in the vestibular sense really enjoy movement in order to receive sensory input to feel alive. They would get a tremendous high from trampolining provided any other sensory deficiencies are taken into account.

- Students who are hypersensitive (over-sensitive) in the vestibular sense find sports difficult as they find it difficult to control their movements. They do find it difficult when their feet are off the ground and find it difficult to stop quickly when asked during trampolining.

- Trampolines are known for helping to maintain coordination and balance thanks to the uneven, bouncy surface. Coordination and balance are both areas students with autism often require help with due to their mobility limitations.

- It is important to keep the whole body in balance and to maintain this balance when learning the movements and changing positions rapidly. Performing complex motor skills, such as those performed on the trampoline, requires a great sense of balance (Vuillerme et al. 2001).

- Students who are hyposensitive (under-sensitive) to smell may be distracted by smells in the room being used. They may even lick things to get a better sense of what those things are.

- Students who are hypersensitive (over-sensitive) to smell are very sensitive to perfumes and after shaves that coaches or support assistants may be using. They may appear to the student to be intense and overpowering.

- Students who are hyposensitive (under-sensitive) to taste are often on the look-out for new tastes to try and tend to put things found in their mouths. Students who take this to extremes eat anything and everything and this is known as pica. You would need to be vigilant as someone who has pica can be an opportunist and you cannot turn your back for a second or start chatting to an adult in the room.

- Students who are hypersensitive (over-sensitive) to taste sometimes chew clothing and objects and may find this a way of calming themselves when they are under stress in a new place.

- Trampolines can also assist with executive functioning and repetitive stimming (see section 7 of the Appendix) where a student is activating the vestibular system because they feel under-stimulated. Jumping on a trampoline is a healthy and enjoyable way to partake in a repetitive activity and a great alternative to other more destructive forms of stimming.

- Playing sports regularly is mostly perceived as valuable to fitness and health, but the development of motor skills requires more discipline and so the technical moves associated with movements in trampolining for example rapidly improve a person's balance. Jumping on the trampoline is an activity which develops motor coordination, aerobic fitness, strength, balance and a sense of rhythm and timing (Heitkamp et al. 2001; Crowther et al. 2007).

- Fine motor skills involve making small movements with small muscles in the body such as fingers, wrists, toes, lips and tongue to do everyday tasks. Trampolines can be used to develop these skills. These tasks can include things like holding items whilst bouncing, reciting numbers or the alphabet whilst bouncing, walking around the trampoline bed on toes, sides of feet, heels.

- Trampolines are also well known for helping to maintain coordination and balance thanks to the uneven, bouncy surface. Fine motor skills, coordination and balance are all areas students with autism often require help with due to their mobility limitations.

- Trampolining can activate the parasympathetic nervous system to decrease anxiety.

- The repetitiveness that comes with gymnastics is sometimes a gift for those with autism. Micah is a national trampoline champion in America, and he is autistic. His father says that Micah can watch videos of himself and other trampolinists for hours and hours to see what he needs to work on and then he tries to perfect it. However, sometimes his obsessive nature is his downfall because he will obsess over a mistake he has made (Donald 2017).

- Anxiety is a common state for students with autism. The sympathetic nervous system is constantly on a state of alert. Bouncing on a trampoline seems to calm students down as the parasympathetic nervous system takes over. This could be why students with autism, and any child for that matter, enjoys simply bouncing on a trampoline – it relaxes them.

- Colleagues have reported increased eye contact and increased interaction with staff delivering the session.

- Anabelle Listic, a Seattle woman with autism, has two trampolines at home and uses them daily to process information and cope with anxiety. 'My moments of true clarity always happen when I'm on my trampoline', Listic said. 'It's like meditation to me'. 'I don't ever want to have to live without jumping on a trampoline', she said. 'When I'm on a trampoline everything feels effortless and makes sense and feels okay' (Egge 2013).

- Anis Ben-Aoun is autistic with limited speech and competes in national mainstream trampolining events in Ontario, Canada. Trampolining has developed his social skills so that he enjoys performing his optional and compulsory routines to spectators. His coach Melynda Outram said, 'I could not teach the spatial awareness that he has. With autism, it's part of the hyper-sensitivity. They're very, very aware in the air' (Brancaccio 2014).

- The Lakeside Centre for Autism in Issaquah, Washington, uses a trampoline for speech, occupational, physical and behavioural therapies. Erica Bigler, an occupational therapist, worked with a five-year-old boy at the centre in 2013 with poor social skills. On a trampoline he was able to share an enjoyable activity and develop increased body awareness around his peers. Bigler said, 'It's one of the only places I see him interact with a peer and sustain attention on a game' (Egge 2013).

Trampolining for students with attention deficit hyperactive disorder (ADHD)

4

What is ADHD?

Attention deficit disorder (ADD) is a neurological disorder. Some students with ADD have comorbid conditions of various types such as severe learning difficulties, and so sometimes the disorder becomes a secondary diagnosis. I have taught and led in special schools for many years and have come across quite a few students with undiagnosed ADD. They find it difficult to attend to lessons but so do those with severe learning difficulties. They don't appear to be listening or concentrating, but then this is not unusual if you have severe learning difficulties. They rarely complete tasks, can be clumsy and find social interaction difficult, due to the time it takes them to process what has been said and deciding on a response. They can be easily distracted, forgetful and lose items. You will regularly get complaints from home that the student has not brought home their school jumper or coat and both school and parent get frustrated by the lack of newsletters arriving home. I have a student in mind as I write. These symptoms are true of most students with severe learning disabilities.

Attention deficit hyperactive disorder (ADHD) on the other hand is far easier to diagnose due to the hyperactivity. You can't overlook someone with ADHD.

Students with ADD are overall not disruptive in school. Students with ADHD usually are. Children can be diagnosed with ADHD with a predominantly inattentive presentation, meaning they are not hyperactive but often parents and some of us in education find that it confuses the issue. However, if a new student is due to attend your school and has a diagnosis of ADHD, it is important that you study the statement to see which subtype it is. In Sweden and other Scandinavian countries, students are diagnosed as having Deficits in Attention, Motor control and Perception (DAMP). DAMP is a combination of ADHD plus DCD (Developmental Coordination Disorder – present in 50% of ADHD cases) (Gillberg & Kadesjo 2003).

In addition to the difficulties someone with ADD has, the hyperactive student is full of energy. They are impulsive and, in my experience, often are unable to stop to think things through. Students that I have had in special schools with ADHD have always suffered with anxiety and mood disorders and low self-esteem. They constantly fidget. They are persistent but this can be a useful trait for them. They are often curious, and it could be why Thomas Edison has been

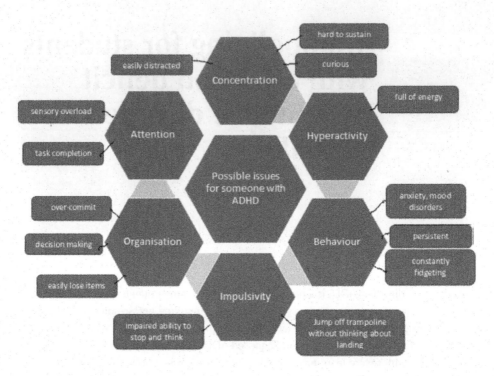

Figure 4.1 Possible issues for someone with Attention Deficit Hyperactive Disorder (ADHD)

described as America's greatest inventor. He is now thought to have had ADHD and was asked to leave school at a very young age.

I have found Neurofeedback has worked for students with ADHD. In fact, one of our students with severe ADHD became a changed child after just two weeks of daily Neurofeedback. The change was so profound his carer came to the school unannounced to thank me for changing her child. She said she had signed the consent forms for him to receive it thinking she was clutching at straws.

She told me that his hyperactivity was so bad he didn't sleep for even an hour at night. As she spoke, I recalled months ago when he had come to ask me for a cardboard box he had seen by the caretaker's room. He had told me he thought he could sleep in it as he couldn't sleep in his bed. Indeed, it was those kinds of conversations that I had had with him that made him a prime candidate for Neurofeedback.

She told me that within days of receiving the half-hour daily sessions, he slept through the night for the first time. She was so used to getting up through the night she stood by his bedroom door at one point enjoying watching him sleep. She told me that the NHS behaviour support team had advised he join a club and she was scared that he might be involved in fights. She started taking him to a club a week after he began the brain training programme. She had to remain at the club. She told me that within 10 minutes of entering the club a boy walked up to him and punched him in the face. She watched expectantly and was shocked but delighted when she heard him tell the boy, 'There are club rules. We are not allowed to fight. I will report you'. And he reported the boy.

Knowing him well I knew she was right when she said that normally he would have hit him back and got into a fight because of his impulsivity.

As a school we noticed his behaviour reports went from between 15–30 incidents a week down to one or two at most. This remarkable change continued for the whole of the two years he remained with us. He moved onto secondary school where I know he is doing well. The Neurofeedback helped him to reason things out and in fact he could be overheard advising other boys to stop and think things through.

Short bursts of work followed by a reward such as a meditation tape for 5 minutes can assist students with ADHD and train them in the art of meditation. The Headspace App is available from App stores and is subscription-based. Headspace also provides sleep casts which aid sleep. There are however free meditation Apps available. Meditation helps them to refuel. TEACCH® tables used with students with autism and explained in chapter 3 have proved useful for short bursts of work in the schools I have managed.

Sleep is a problem and parents have told me that some students find that they go to sleep better with white noise in the background and wearing an eye mask.

I can also recommend giving students with ADHD a blank page book at the beginning of the term and encouraging them to doodle, draw, scribble or write in it when their brain is working too fast for them to be able to concentrate on anything. It is their book and private to them and they can throw it away or take it home when it is full and they can ask for a new one.

In special schools we tend to have daily and weekly schedules and these help students with ADHD to focus. It is an executive function skill and a skill that they find difficult without some kind of scaffold. If you have students with ADHD in a mainstream school, then I would recommend helping them to schedule their week and each day. It can be just a personal timetable or keeping a journal or a 'To Do' List but they should be allowed to take it home. Just keep a copy in school in case they leave it at home by mistake. They depend on them so much they will not have left it at home on purpose. If a brother or sister has hid it to be mean, then you are their guardian angel.

Some of us when we work need complete quiet but often students with ADHD want background music that suits the tempo of the work to keep them focussed. This needs a discussion on appropriate music with the student and of course headphones if the music is being used in a classroom so that others are not distracted. If we don't give students the stimulation that they require in order to work, then they will find it some other way.

Trampolining

One of the biggest differences between ADD and ADHD is obviously the fact that a person with ADHD is full of energy. What better way to use and direct that energy than on the trampoline? Hyperactivity may decrease as a student finds a healthy way to channel their energy. Exercise is not only good for the body but is also good for the brain as it releases endorphins and boosts dopamine. People diagnosed with ADHD are known to have low dopamine levels. Exercise stimulates neurotransmitters in the brain that help us to focus. This happens immediately after exercise so that we then feel more productive. Exercise also helps us sleep better and as sleep can be a problem for those with ADHD, it makes sense for parents and teachers to encourage exercise to become a habit. Finally, exercise promotes neurogenesis, which is the growth of new brain cells.

If trampoline or mini trampoline sessions are not currently available at school, then it would be a good idea for a parent of a child with ADHD to try out a local club or trampoline park to see if trampolining is the exercise that appeals to them. If it is, then you could purchase a garden trampoline or a mini trampoline so that your child gets the brain boost that they need. Breathing in fresh air whilst trampolining gives additional health benefits.

The trampoline sequence cards for dyslexia in chapter 7 can be used with all students and they are useful for those with ADHD because they add structure to the session reminding them when to stop. They also aid them in organisation and can stop them rushing through routines. We have to remember that competitive trampolining is a relatively short high-energy exercise. I have found that with a group of students who are able to take part at this level that the most important part of the session is learning to wait your turn and learn to work as a team so that you get a second or even third turn on the trampoline during that session. Session cards can be used in school or at home. Students and children with ADHD need routine.

There are trampoline rules in chapter 9 that should be enlarged to poster size and put up by your trampoline and you may wish to issue penalties (think football and yellow cards) for anyone not following the rules. The reason for the rules is that the trampoline can be dangerous if the rules aren't followed. Students with ADHD do not intentionally decide not to follow rules and in my experience, they just need to know why they can't do something. Trampoline rules should make this clear. Going through trampoline rules should be the first trampoline lesson. I would suggest that in the first session rules are explained and students watch a demonstration and are told that they will have a timed session at the end of the lesson to bounce on the trampoline. A thoughtful assistant may have brought the student's favourite music to bounce to. Students need to learn to respect the rules and to realise that a trampoline session is not a free for all that it might be on a home trampoline. Sand timers are a useful tool for students with ADHD when they are working on the trampoline. You can get 1-minute, 3-minute and 5-minute sand timers so that they can see they have had their minutes of music and bounce time.

Students with ADHD are known to hyperfocus. This means that they can become engrossed in something that interests them to such an extent that they forget to attend to basic routines such as eating meals on time, brushing teeth etc and must be constantly reminded. However, some of the greatest inventions have come from those able to hyperfocus and some of the greatest sports people have or had ADHD. Michael Phelps, winner of numerous Olympic gold medals, was diagnosed with ADHD at the age of nine. I know of a trampoline club where two of its current young members have ADHD and both are competing in the national competition. There is nothing to say that they can't become Olympic champions at the sport if they have that as their goal.

Some people with ADHD receive medication and this needs to be borne in mind. At all my schools we have made sure that parents have completed a consent form and a screening form. I have included photocopiable forms in chapter 7.

To assist a student with ADHD to become organised when attending trampoline competitions is essential or they could easily be disqualified. You will need to devise a checklist for them to tick off as they prepare. It could be something that you as a trampoline coach/therapist put into practice as soon as they start attending your class. This not only helps them with their ADHD, it makes life a little easier for you too. There is a saying known as the seven Ps and I will quote the toned-down version that is used all the time in special schools because planning is vital when dealing with children with learning differences. It is 'Prior proper planning prevents painfully poor production'.

Some ideas that we used for supporting students who have ADHD by use of the trampoline and/or mini trampoline are:

- Tick-off sheet for trampoline schedule to aid student in self-management and organisation.
- Use the Stop, Think, Do approach whilst coaching trampolining (more information can be found at www.stopthinkdo.com/prog_core.php). You may perhaps use a yellow card which the student has been taught to recognise means Stop. You then use a single word such as 'Think' encouraging the student to self-talk /motivate themselves to concentrate on their performance. Do this when they put their plan of action into place.
- Trampoline Rules displayed prominently. Consequences for failure to follow. Instant rewards for keeping to rules.
- Some students with ADHD find that certain types of music help them to pay attention and will bounce in time to the beat.
- Sequence cards such as those in chapter 7 can help the student focus on the task at hand.
- Allow fidget toys for students while they are waiting for their turn on the trampoline.
- Trampoline programmes with certificates encourage students with ADHD to achieve. This book recommends the Winstrada programme or the British Gymnastics trampoline programme. Both have certificates. Clubs often have their own programmes or use one of these two and clubs have competitions and other reward systems in place.
- Students with ADHD are risk takers, impulsive and often ingenious. These can be positive traits in the world of trampolining. Remember to positively encourage their sessions as they take part. They need constant positive reinforcement.
- There is a trampoline therapy session sheet in chapter 7. This is a useful tracking sheet to track whether trampolining has benefitted the student.
- Have the student practice stillness before dismounting from trampoline. This is an expectation in competitions. If the student gets into the habit of doing so, it won't come as such a shock.
- Be strict with the number of bounces required. Let the student know that an extra bounce in a competition penalises them and deductions are made.
- You may wish to score trampoline sessions out of 10 if you are preparing the student for competitions.
- If a student is going to enter competitions, ensure that you go through all the rules and expectations and really prepare them.

5 | Trampolining for students with dyslexia and students with dyspraxia

What is dyslexia?

I have a post-graduate diploma in dyslexia studies, and I have run centres for those with dyslexia for many years. My father was dyslexic. Dyslexia is when someone finds it difficult to read and write. They may find it difficult to match letters to the sounds they hear, which is called a lack of phonological awareness. They can have great difficulty with spelling and may write letters back to front or upside down or even mirror write. They may spell the same word differently every time that they try to write it.

They may have trouble telling left from right. Listening to and having to remember a list of directions can be particularly upsetting for them as they may then not be able to follow those directions once the person has finished giving them.

Information processing can take longer and so more thinking time needs to be given. Students with dyslexia must work harder than the ordinary student to decode words. Therefore, it is always important to ensure a proper diagnosis of dyslexia is sought and given as exam boards allow extra time for people who have a diagnosis. Organisation is another area they can struggle with.

Most dyslexics have poor short-term memories and memorising sequences can be difficult.

If they enjoy using a keyboard or a dictation App, then this can help enormously with 'written work' as the handwriting task can be very onerous because they often realise words don't look right and they may cross out words and retry many times in a piece of writing. A spell check is a great help. There have been many support tools over the years produced to support those with dyslexia and they are constantly being revised and updated. Now that the technological age has exploded into our midst, students today have more immediate support than ever before.

I have recently had staff trained in delivering Neurofeedback. Neurofeedback has been proven to help the brain charge up areas that are not working and create new brainwave patterns. The feedback can reinforce selected brainwave patterns while discouraging others. Neurofeedback has no negative side effects. The person who delivered the training to staff at the school I led came to our National Conference on Therapeutic Interventions held at the school in 2016. He told me that his wife had, like me, worked with people who had dyslexia for many years. He told me that she found that Neurofeedback had a quicker effect on her students, and they showed more

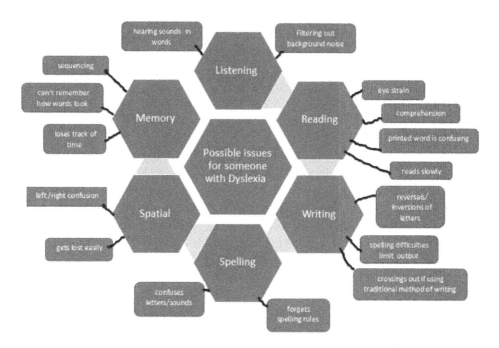

Figure 5.1 Possible issues for someone with Dyslexia

progress through using Neurofeedback than using the traditional methods of teaching those with dyslexia. I don't know of any comparative research, but it is something worth bearing in mind. I do know that we have had success using it with students with ADHD and as sessions were fully booked up, we did not find time to do that research with our students who had dyslexia as a secondary diagnosis (their primary diagnosis being autism or ADHD or Severe learning difficulties).

Just as everyone with autism is different so is everyone with dyslexia. I have worked with dyslexics who were extroverts, who were the jokers of the class, drawing attention away from their difficulties. I have worked also with many dyslexics who were introverts, who hated any attention on themselves because they felt that most of the attention they got was about their failings.

Just because they can find traditional teaching methods difficult does not mean that they have a low IQ and so they are often very aware of their own failings and this can lead to frustration which can lead to behaviour problems. It is now widely known that one in four persons in prison suffers with dyslexia (Anderson 2019). In 1999 when I was deputy head of a secondary special school the head teacher had an unexpected visitor to the school. She informed the visitor that I would be able to help him and I was called to her office. Apparently he believed he had undiagnosed dyslexia and I agreed in that office to do an assessment.

It was only later, just prior to the assessment, that I was informed he had been in prison. They may do things differently, but they are often very creative. Richard Branson is such an example.

Steve Chinn is a pioneer teacher and researcher in the field of dyslexia and dyscalculia. He has written award-winning books and given award-winning presentations on both subjects. I well recall going to a conference he spoke at in the 1990s when he referred to the two different types of thinking styles – the inchworm and the grasshopper. He said that basically one style (the inchworm) is formulaic and sequential and the other is intuitive and holistic (the grasshopper) and that we need to adopt different strategies to teach students with different thinking styles to achieve the greatest effectiveness.

It goes without saying that we all can have some of the traits of dyslexia. It is only when we have most or all of them that we can be classed as dyslexic and only by undergoing a proper assessment can we get a certified diagnosis.

Trampolining

In the summer holidays in the 1990s the Gwent Dyslexia Centre that I used to help manage ran summer schools. We would have access to a trampoline, and I had heard at the time of some good work done with students who had dyslexia using the trampoline in Australia. So, we tried it and found it successful. Basically, the students started off practicing basic trampoline routines and then would have to recall a sequence of them. The sequences could start off small and increase in length depending on the student's desire and ability.

Carl Delacato in his book *The Diagnosis and Treatment of Speech and Reading Problems* (1963) writes about the benefits trampolining was found to have. Delacato's research states that 'The results were most revealing and explain the effectiveness of the trampoline'. He wrote that 'the repeated change from weightlessness to strong deceleration provides a gravitational pull rarely experienced by children. It results in new and constantly changing stimulation of consecutive neural levels of the brain towards greater neurological organisation'. Carl Delacato teamed up with Glenn Doman, a pioneer in the field of child brain development, to develop the Doman Delacato Patterning Therapy (see section 8 of the Appendix). This therapy aimed to address the underlying neurological causes of learning difficulties, such as dyslexia, rather than the individual symptoms.

I decided, based on my research, to draw up picture sequence cards and written sequence for those who wished to use them, and they could choose an easy card or a hard card and score points if the students wanted to be competitive. The student was asked to memorise the card and do the sequence when preoccupied with bouncing up and down and keeping their balance. As trampolining was such fun, they really enjoyed this difficult task and we saw an improvement in their short-term memory, organisation and enhanced consolidation. The trampoline can help those with dyslexia specifically with spatial awareness, developing listening skills and memory.

Rules for using the trampoline are included in chapter 9. It is very important for all students to follow these rules. A scheme of work and lesson plans for trampolining are also included. They can be adapted so that you work on the ideas suggested in this chapter which are more specifically for students with dyslexia or dyspraxia.

- Remember to give praise and positive encouragement.
- Ensure the student is in the centre of the trampoline.
- Start off with little steps and increase as the student develops confidence.
- Don't give too many verbal or written instructions at one time.
- Ask the student to repeat the instructions to you so that you know they understand and so that they reinforce them to memory.
- Give students plenty of time to change and include this time in lesson planning as it is an important part of their learning.

Some ideas and benefits of supporting students who are dyslexic by use of the trampoline and/or mini trampoline are:

- Experiential learning is empowering.
- Bounce on the trampoline to a count of five, then STOP.
- Follow a trampoline sequence card (see chapter 7 for copiable cards). The cards do not have too many instructions and have visuals for those who struggle with reading. You would ask the student if they understood the sequence and to repeat it to you before they attempt it so that they remember it more easily.
- Bounce on the mini trampoline, say what is shown you on your left.
- Bounce on the mini trampoline, say what is shown you on your right.
- Bounce on the mini trampoline, say what is shown in front of you.
- Students are shown an image of a car and a house. They are asked to remember those two images. They are then asked to bounce and say the opposite of what picture they are shown. If shown the car, they must say 'house' and vice versa. This develops short-term memory as well as critical thinking skills.
- The coach demonstrates quarter-twist and half-twist jumps whilst the assistant calls out the direction left or right; the coach stands behind the student touching their shoulder and turning with the student as the assistant calls out the direction and required turn. Once the student is confident, the coach leaves the trampoline and the student twists left or right according to the direction called out. As well as developing spatial awareness, this encourages healthy risk taking.
- Bounce while spelling sight words aloud.
- Bounce while sounding out words posted on the wall in front of you.
- Bounce while counting or reciting the alphabet.

What is dyspraxia?

Some years ago, I ran dyslexic centres and some of the students who attended were found to also have dyspraxia. I got involved with the local dyspraxia foundation and accompanied them on a summer break one year. The physiotherapists and occupational therapists who attended the camping holiday were keen to encourage self-help skills. I found that we had to adapt our teaching methods to ensure that we catered to their needs.

Dyspraxics can have difficulty with spatial awareness. They are usually disorganised. They have been called clumsy children in the past as they can trip and fall over more easily and bump into things and so can appear to be accident-prone. It is known as developmental coordination disorder (DCD) in some countries.

Dyspraxia is when messages from the brain to the body are not getting through properly. This then affects the student's ability to plan, organise, coordinate and perform actions and movements. It affects fine motor skills, and this can lead to the student finding difficulty with being able to dress themselves as well as gripping a pencil or using an ordinary keyboard on a computer. Dyspraxia also affects gross motor skills so that it may take them longer to learn to crawl, walk and toilet train. They may not be able to run, hop or jump at the age their peers can. Riding a bike or taking

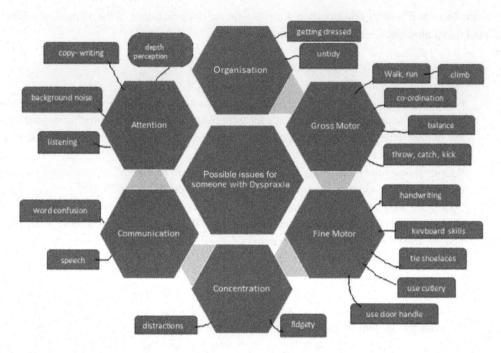

Figure 5.2 Possible issues for someone with Dyspraxia

part in sport may be challenging for the dyspraxic student. An early diagnosis can help provide the right kind of support. Dyspraxia can affect any child of any ability. It can also vary in its severity.

Because we repeat certain movements every day a person who is dyspraxic may improve in those areas over time. This doesn't mean that the person is no longer dyspraxic.

For dyspraxics both writing and typing can be difficult and there are resources available to schools to assist students in overcoming these difficulties. Riding a bike and taking part in sport can be difficult and so it is important for a physiotherapist to assess the student and to give the school and trampoline coach guidance.

Motor planning also affects speech and so students with dyspraxia may have speech delay and will need input from a speech therapist.

Students with dyspraxia may have poor depth perception. Good depth perception prevents us from bumping into things. It also lets you determine how fast a ball is coming towards you, or how fast a car is coming towards you. I would always recommend that if you are a parent of a child who has poor depth perception (there are easy tests for it on YouTube), then visit an optometrist and ask for a test using the Howard-Dolman apparatus. There are now specialist school vision opticians around the UK and abroad who can assess your child. Please follow the link to find out more: www.sportvision.co.uk/schoolvision/home.aspx

Trampolining

Students with dyspraxia benefit from using the trampoline. A study in 2015 concluded that balance training with the use of a trampoline can be an effective way for improving functional outcomes in students with developmental coordination disorder (DCD) and can be recommended as an alternative mode of physical activity (Giagazoglou et al. 2015).

The Fox Vision Development Center uses a trampoline for training the eyes (see http://www.foxvisiondevelopment.com). Vision can be improved by completing challenging visual exercises such as jumping on a trampoline because this stimulates the vestibular system which then stimulates easier eye movements.

The trampoline increases the G force, which is the force created by the body as a result of gravity. When you jump on a trampoline or mini trampoline, you accelerate and decelerate on each jump. All 638 muscles in the body alternately flex and relax, resulting in strength and vitality.

Repetition of a trampoline movement will support the student in developing new skills. At our summer schools we found that it was important for students with dyspraxia that they are not shown how to do something but are given support by the trampoline coach to learn the skill for themselves as they learn better by doing the action. Trampolining exercises the jumper's reflexes as the body must constantly adjust in position in order to maintain balance. It may also increase postural muscle tone as a defence from falling over on the trampoline.

You can follow the Winstrada trampoline programme or the British Gymnastics programme and alter them to suit your needs, or you can, as we did, develop your own specific trampoline programme for particular students. You can always alternate between them and if you find that a programme works best then follow that. If the student begins to excel at trampolining, then the next step would be to encourage the parents to find a suitable club or trampoline park where the student can develop those skills further and maybe even compete.

Some ideas that we used for supporting students who are dyspraxic by use of the trampoline are:

- Train the brain to cope with doing two things at once. Keep a balloon in the air.
- Balance/bounce on a trampoline and throw/catch a bean bag.
- Students with dyspraxia can have poor depth perception and appear clumsy. They can have problems with throwing and catching because they can't see clearly, and vision is blurred. Sometimes throwing a ball or bean bag is included in work on a mini trampoline in the classroom in order to develop this skill in students.
- Download a free interactive metronome from www.imusic-school.com; the student listens to the beat and then jumps to the beat.
- Hands and knees bounces (many students with dyspraxia never learned to crawl – crawling strengthens the arms, wrists, hands and upper body), hands and knees moving around the trampoline.
- Pushing oneself up from tummy position and moving around the trampoline.
- Bunny hop on the trampoline, strengthening the shoulders.
- Bounce, drop to knees and back to standing bounce position.
- Bounce, drop to seat position and back to standing bounce position.
- Walk on heels on the trampoline bed.
- Walk on the insides of the feet on the trampoline bed.
- Walk on the outsides of the feet on the trampoline bed.
- Jump with feet together, jump with feet apart.

6 | Trampolining in special schools

Many Special schools throughout the UK deliver trampolining in some form or other. The British Gymnastics Association offers training via the Teachers' Trampoline Awards which consists of two parts. Part One must be completed before progressing to Part Two. Part One and Part Two courses may run concurrently, consisting of a four-day delivery.

In order to be eligible to attend the Teachers' Trampoline Awards, a candidate must be either a qualified PE teacher, or a trainee PE teacher, or teachers who hold a current UKCC Level 2 (or higher) BG coaching award, or equivalent.

The Teachers' Trampoline Awards train teachers in all kinds of jumps, twists and somersaults and these techniques would not usually be taught in a Special school. However, other parts of the Award programme such as how to set up and dismantle a trampoline, health and safety issues and early levels that you may teach would be extremely useful. If a teacher has the necessary qualifications and is keen to go on the course, I would encourage it.

Rebound Therapy.org is the official UK body and international consultancy for a trampoline programme known as Rebound Therapy for special needs. Some Special schools send their staff to be trained so that they can provide the therapy themselves. The basic course is a two-day certificated course. Other schools bring in trained therapists to deliver the therapy. Rebound Therapy is suitable for all students including those who are in wheelchairs or who have PMLD. Winstrada.com provides free development scheme resources. Grades 1–3 are ideal for Rebound Therapy and were compiled in association with ReboundTherapy.org. It is not just schools that have staff trained.

The NHS has many of its physiotherapists trained in the therapy. If you have a physiotherapist who is trained attached to your school, then you can ask them to deliver the therapy to your students. Alternatively, you can ask them to be involved in the assessment of students taking part in the therapy.

I have to say that most students that we have had in recent years remained on Winstrada Proficiency Grade 1 for their entire school life. However, they did not work just on that specific therapy whilst on the trampoline as the trampoline was used as a vehicle for cross-curricular learning.

Trampolining is a way for students to learn without realising they are learning. I have worked at several Special schools and all those schools had their staff trained to deliver Rebound Therapy.

Pen Coch was a brand-new school when it opened 10 years ago. When we opened, a member of staff was trained to be a trainer of the therapy by Rebound Therapy.org so that as many members of staff as possible could be trained to deliver the therapy. As a peer inspector for Estyn, Her Majesty's Inspectorate for Education and Training in Wales, I have observed trampolining being delivered in different Special schools. All those schools delivered the therapy. Information on training and resources available can be found at www.reboundtherapy.org

The Sir Stanley Matthews Foundation has been involved with Rebound Therapy for three years, providing grants to schools so that staff may be trained in the therapy. I recently visited Tir Morfa, a Special school in Rhyl which caters to students with a wide range of additional learning needs aged between 3 and 19 years. They have already benefitted from the Sir Stanley Matthews grant by having two members of staff trained. The school is now following up the latest project offered by the Foundation, which is training the trainers for Rebound Therapy. On completion of the Therapy Course, the trainers will become Sir Stanley Matthews Rebound Therapy Coaches and will be expected to represent the Foundation with values that were part of Sir Stanley's life. For information on how you can get a grant, go to www.sirstanleymatthews.co.uk

Some Special schools don't have staff with any trampolining qualification and use the trampoline as a vehicle for delivering a Sensory Curriculum. Some Special schools have their physiotherapist

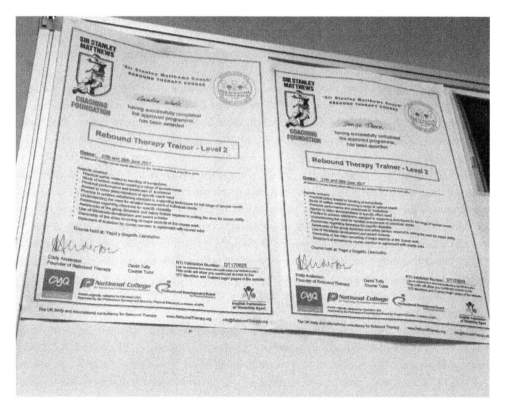

Figure 6.1 Sir Stanley Matthews Certificates

deliver trampolining to their students. The physiotherapist may deliver an individual physiotherapy programme using the trampoline. When I opened a new Special school in 2009, the lead phys- iotherapist was very keen to ensure the school had a trampoline and managed to get a new full- sized free-standing trampoline for the school. The trampoline was used extensively by our trained Rebound Therapists to deliver the therapy and also by the physiotherapists who delivered physio- therapy programmes using the trampoline. We also allowed them to use the trampoline to deliver physiotherapy to students from other schools outside of our school hours. Physiotherapists support students to develop and maintain their mobility skills, joint range of movement, muscle strength and motor skills. They can be relied upon to give advice on whether the trampoline is a suitable vehicle to deliver the programmes that they have devised for individual students and confirm the appropriateness of the exercises.

Physiotherapists will also train and support teaching assistants in the delivery of these pro- grammes on the trampoline. They will provide equipment, such as the Peanut Roll (see chapter 2 for a photo of this piece of equipment) and show staff how it can be used on the trampoline.

Therapeutic trampolining is popular in Special needs schools and is becoming increasingly popular in mainstream schools within special need's units. This could be because the trampoline is a piece of apparatus that virtually all people, regardless of their abilities, can access benefit from and enjoy.

Some Special schools, who do not have their own trampoline, use the local trampoline club or park where a trained coach delivers trampolining such as Pear Tree School in Preston. Some Special schools, such as Greenfields in Merthyr and Hen Felin in Pentre, have the coaches from the local trampoline club deliver sessions at their school using the school trampoline. It shows the determination of these schools to provide trampolining for their students in order to enhance their physical and emotional wellbeing.

Some schools do not have a room set aside for a trampoline and must set up and dismantle the trampoline every time they need to use it. I have inspected schools where they often have no choice but to use the school hall which can also serve as the school canteen, the school sports hall, the school assembly hall etc. As a school hall is in constant use, this means that trampoline sessions may be limited to once or twice a week in those schools. From a health and safety per- spective, setting up and dismantling regularly is not ideal. I have visited some schools recently that have their trampoline set up in the hall and dismantled daily and they did not want to be photographed. They all adhered to health and safety regulations. See chapter 9 for more informa- tion on health and safety and risk assessment. Using the trampoline for such a small amount of time can either appear as paying lip service to the sport/therapy or can be seen as at least trying to offer it to a few instead of not at all. In most of the schools I visited not all students are given the opportunity to use the trampoline as time is limited and the schools have to prioritise. Who decides who should have the opportunity and how often? How can we give every student in a Special school the opportunity?

As a previous headteacher of a Special school and part of senior management teams before that, I am very aware of the benefits trampolining has given to students with Profound and Multiple Learning Difficulties, students with Autism, Attention Deficit Hyperactive Disorder and Severe Learning Difficulties. As a previous manager of a Dyslexic and Dyspraxic Centre, I also know the benefits those students got from using the trampoline. Nowadays trampolining has become more accessible because of the mini trampoline version.

Many schools, both Special and mainstream, use mini trampolines to help control anxiety and relieve the build-up of stress. They can be used to support individuals to improve their levels of attention and focus in the classroom. Opportunities to move and participate for 10- to 15-minute sessions will allow students to improve their brain processing efficiency and engage them, making them ready to learn. Mini trampolines are included in sensory circuits that are now used in schools that have pupils with sensory processing disorder or autism. Sensory circuits involve three types of activities; when used in order they can be effective in supporting individuals to improve their levels of attention and focus in the classroom. Circuits are organised into three main sections:

Alerting To provide vestibular stimulation – activities that make the head change direction rapidly, e.g. bouncing, jumping, skipping, step-ups and spinning.

Organising The second set of activities requires multi-sensory processing and balance. They should provide motor challenges to the child.

Calming The third set of activities should be those that calm the child such as deep pressure, proprioceptive input and heavy work. It is very important to provide input that ensures that as a student leaves the circuit and enters the classroom, they are as calm and centred as possible.

Sensory circuits are highly effective for students with sensory processing problems and can help them to regulate their sensory needs. Schools can set up their own sensory circuits using equipment that they possibly already have in their PE store.

Mini trampolines are also called trampets in some areas of the UK and are often referred to as rebounders in the US.

If you go to www.cpft.nhs.uk and look for Sensory Motor Circuit, you will find that the Cambridge and Peterborough NHS provide you with an example that you can copy. It is based on the resources they had and includes a trampet. We based our sensory circuit on it in my last school but adapted it to fit with the resources we had. It has been devised by occupational therapists and the mini trampoline suggestions can be used on their own within a class setting. Please see chapter 7 for mini trampoline routine ideas that I have devised in the past.

Both Pen Coch Special school and Tir Morfa Special school have designated trampoline rooms. Both have free-standing trampolines set up in these rooms. Both have overhead hoists installed in these rooms.

Both schools have made use of available space. In both schools only those students who are non-ambulant can use the trampoline due to the height restrictions.

Schools have been using trampolines since they were invented in the 1960s and became popular. The construction hasn't changed greatly but new schools are having their trampolines embedded in the floor. This is because it is a safer and easier alternative to above-ground trampolines. There is no need for the many spotters required around a free-standing trampoline. Spotters are there to help stop a student from falling off the trampoline. Pen Coch was completed in 2009 and I became headteacher of the new school. Unfortunately, I wasn't involved in its design with Wynne Construction or I would have ensured that it had a trampoline sunken in the floor.

The physiotherapy service donated a trampoline from Continental Sports to the school. Initially the trampoline had to be set up in the hall when the hall wasn't being used for assemblies, dinners, other sports etc. and so this was limited to two or three sessions a week. Due to the hall's

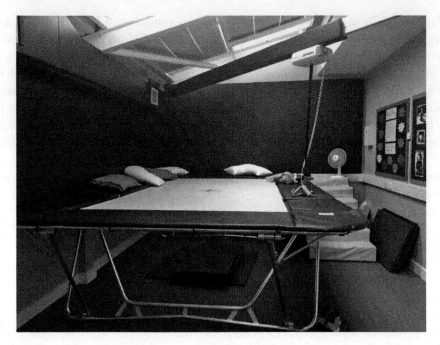

Figure 6.2 Ysgol Tir Morfa trampoline room

construction, the trampoline could only be set up in a certain space. The local authority's Sports coordinator informed us that it couldn't be used by students who were ambulant due to the height restrictions. An outdoor trampoline was embedded in the school playground for those who couldn't use the indoor trampoline. The outdoor trampoline had the added advantage of being able to take students in their wheelchairs accompanied by an assistant or teacher. However, trampoline lessons weren't delivered on the outdoor trampoline. A different room in school was found to house the free-standing trampoline permanently. Only students who would not be standing and jumping on the trampoline could use it, due again to height restrictions.

A few schools are lucky enough to have trampolines embedded in the floor. Hafod Lon in Penrhyndeudraeth is one of those schools. It also has an overhead screen for visual and auditory stimulation.

The school has the addition of a screen outside the room for other staff to observe the session without interrupting the session.

I visited Hafod Lon on several occasions and was told that they incorporate trampolining into their curriculum as a tool to enhance children's learning from a physical viewpoint, but also, in terms of their communication skills. I was told, 'The children are hugely motivated to spend time on the trampoline, and the fact the trampoline is sunken means that all children can safely access without the associated risks of a standard setup'.

A dedicated trampoline room with an embedded trampoline in the floor enables the school to access this great resource without the need for lifting lids, opening and closing trampolines, laying padding out and all the preparation that normally comes with trampoline use. It also means that potentially every student in the school can use the trampoline. In my opinion this is how it should be for every Special school.

Figure 6.3 Hafod Lon's trampoline embedded in the floor

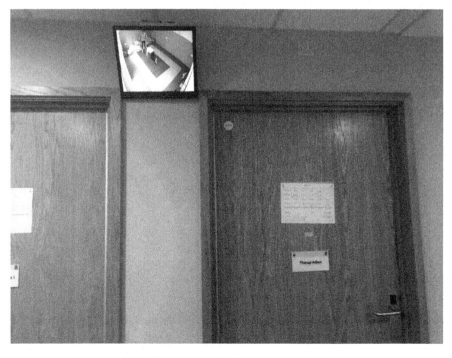

Figure 6.4 Hafod Lon trampoline room exterior with viewing TV

The staff at Hafod Lon have attended the train the trainer course to ensure that all staff can be trained to deliver Rebound Therapy too.

All the schools I visited follow the Winstrada Trampoline Programme as well as their own programmes. Everything is downloadable from www.winstrada.com

Hafod Lon has adapted the Winstrada programme with the use of symbols so that students may understand what is expected of them.

Hafod Lon is leading the way in the use of the trampoline as a therapeutic provision. In schools the trampoline is a fun way to develop physical skills and promote fitness. It is also used as a cross-curricular resource. It aids social skills by encouraging turn-taking, musical preferences and orientation.

All the schools I visited teach literacy and numeracy either incidentally or purposefully during their trampoline sessions. Trampolining can be the medium our students use to help them communicate. A student is often expected to sign or communicate that they want 'more'. They may be required to count several bounces, use a familiar object or picture to communicate, respond to a staff member. I have evidence of improved listening and concentration as well as substantiating a physiotherapy programme (Anderson 2015). Some schools use local trampoline clubs and

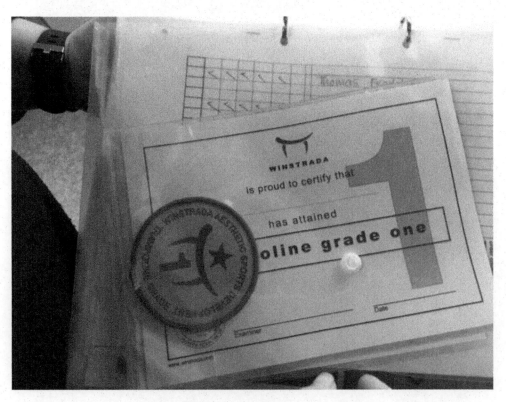

Figure 6.5 Winstrada Certificate and badges

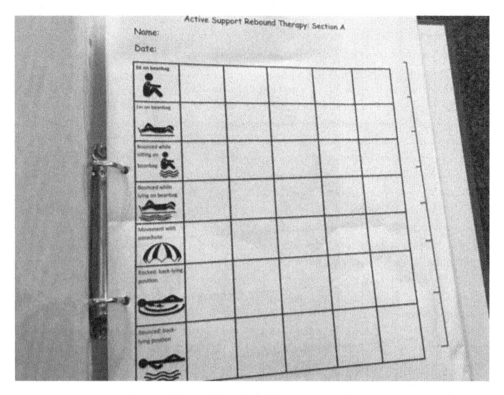

Figure 6.6 Adapted Programme

parks to deliver trampolining by qualified staff and it is a more cost-effective way for that school to ensure its students have the opportunity.

Pen Coch uses a standard trampoline, and also mini trampolines are used regularly in sensory circuits devised for students with autism. Participation in a short sensory circuit encourages the development of the student's sensory processing skills. The alerting session provides vestibular and proprioceptive stimulation while they bounce several times on the mini trampoline. The organising session of a circuit can include balancing on the mini trampoline. The organising section can also be a time when a sequence of trampoline movements is followed to support motor sensory processing. The mini trampoline has provided our students with an outlet for excess energy whilst helping them to control their anxieties and relieve the build-up of stress. Students have shown an increased level of calm, confidence and spatial awareness through using them. Sand timers are used so that a student knows when their time on the mini trampoline is up.

In all the schools I visited staff delivering trampolining had a specific kit that they change into and students usually changed. See chapter 9 for more information.

Mini trampolines are also becoming popular in schools as a group-based therapy. In these sessions groups of students take part in mini trampolining sometimes to improve their sensory processing skills as in the sensory circuit format but also in developing a sense of belonging with other students. All students work on their own trampoline islands and so they can work at their own pace with their own personal space bubble around them.

They are used in some schools to improve cognitive development, co-ordinate and sequence different movement patterns, social skills and self-confidence. It is a learning experience that's fun, rewarding and motivating. In addition, it has been proven that trampoline exercises can help students in promoting the level of health and motor performance (Aalizadeh 2016).

The STAR institute in America runs such mini trampoline sessions. The Rebounders sessions are run by experienced occupational therapists who have been involved in two research projects for students aged 4 to 10 with Sensory Processing Disorder. The findings so far suggest that group trampoline classes may be effective in improving motor difficulties of children with and without Sensory Processing Disorder. Other changes were also noticeable in the students who took part. These were an improvement in self-confidence, self-esteem and increased interactions and socialisation among the participants (spdstar.org 2019).

Cook School in Western Australia is a Special school that uses mini trampolines to enable students to use endorphins to help them self-regulate their emotions. The principal Dave Hobson said that time out doesn't work but 'We've found that we can get a much better result by the student having a jump on the trampoline. The heavy muscle movement, the repetitiveness of the jump and the heavy endorphin boost helps them think about the issue in a different way. We can have a talk with them and get them back in the classroom and learning much faster than consequence-based punitive methods used in the past' (Singhal 2018).

Bounce Beyond is a mini-rebounder workshop provider that works in schools in the UK with both small and large groups of students that have learning difficulties. It delivers therapeutic trampolining, competition trampolining and coaching as well as exercise and wellbeing classes. If you are interested in finding out more, go to www.bouncebeyond.co.uk

Things to bear in mind when purchasing a mini trampoline for a school are the following:

Mini trampolines are cheaper than full-sized trampolines.
Mini trampolines can be more easily stored as they can fold flat and are obviously smaller than the traditional trampoline.
Mini trampolines can be used singly in classrooms or as a group activity in a hall. Ensure you purchase good-quality, quiet mini trampolines.

Watch my previous school deliver a trampoline session at: www.youtube.com/watch?v=5apkQl Mbgfl&t=629s

Trampolining essentials

This chapter provides photocopiable materials for you to adapt for use in your school, club, park or home.

1   Trampoline Cards Figures 7.1–7.6

The Trampoline cards on the following pages were used with students who had dyslexia. They were devised at the time to develop sequencing skills and short-term memory. They were used during summer clubs and so do not have schemes of work or lesson plans. The idea for sequencing trampoline moves into short sessions that the student with dyslexia verbally repeats to the teacher came from Australia. I am afraid I no longer have the reference for that except that the teacher's name was Rob. He did not suggest cards but we found they acted as a prompt and you may copy them or just use the idea to make ones more relevant to the individual student.

As there were several students the time was limited, and they had to learn about turn-taking and spotting as well as being able to have a go on the trampoline. The cards can be photo-copied, and the number of bounces increased so that you have an increased number of cards. I started off with a small amount of bounces to develop the other skills British Gymnastics required for Proficiency level 1 – waiting in turn and showing good behaviour around the trampoline as we would have a small group of students attending the session.

It is very important from the earliest stages for students to learn when to stop as it is an important aspect of trampoline competitions.

Students are not expected to read the cards, though they may do so. Students are often visual learners and the pictures could mean more once explained. The teacher will read out the expected sequences in the hope that the student will remember them. Therefore, the sequences are short. The aim was for success. The teacher may decide to demonstrate first. It is worth explaining to students that although their time on the trampoline may seem short, it is possible that students may get more than one go on the trampoline during the session.

2   Template for leaflet advertising Trampoline Therapy

This leaflet was created to advertise trampolining benefits to parents and visitors. We kept leaflets at the reception area. We also sent copies home to parents.

3   Contraindications for Trampoline Therapy
    It is worth sharing the contraindications with parents and with anyone who wishes to take part in trampolining at the school.

4   Therapeutic Trampolining Screening Form
    This form is vitally important. It must be completed and signed by parent/carer/doctor/physiotherapist to ensure that every care has been taken before a person is allowed on the trampoline.

5   Individual Session Recording Form
    This is one form that may be used to record a session of trampolining. The emphasis is on evidence. This also refers to Routes for Learning (RfL). RfL is material that supports practitioners in assessing the early communication and cognitive skills of students with PMLD. Go to https://hwb.gov.wales/curriculum-for-wales-2008/routesforlearning for a downloadable assessment booklet and for more information.

6   Trampoline Therapy Session Sheet
    A form used to record a session with the emphasis on wellbeing and next steps.

7   Scheme of Work – Trampolining for students with Additional Learning Needs (ALN). This scheme of work is based on the BG Award level 1.

8   Lesson plans based on Trampolining ALN scheme of work.

9   Scheme of Work for Trampolining – Students with Profound and Multiple Learning Difficulties (PMLD). This scheme is based on Winstrada Rebound Therapy level 1.

10 Lesson plans based on Trampolining PMLD Scheme of Work.

11 Communication Table for Trampolining.
    This document was produced by staff at Hafod Lon. Copies should be laminated and available for use in the trampoline room.

12 Communication Placemat.
    This placemat has sections for parent and teacher to complete. The central box could contain a photo of the student. These are working documents that are updated as and when changes take place. The parent has the final approval of this document and a smaller version for the student's travel escort and driver (named a Taxi passport) is then also made.

13 Individual Education Plan (IEP). All students with ALN should have an IEP. An IEP will set the targets for the term. IEPs tend to be targets broken down from the Annual targets to ensure that the year's targets, set at the Annual Review, are met.

14 Mini Trampoline Cards Figure 7.9 These can be photocopied, laminated and cut out as individual cards to use with students.

15 Sensory, Therapeutic and Physical Wellbeing Policy.

16 Therapeutic Trampolining Policy.

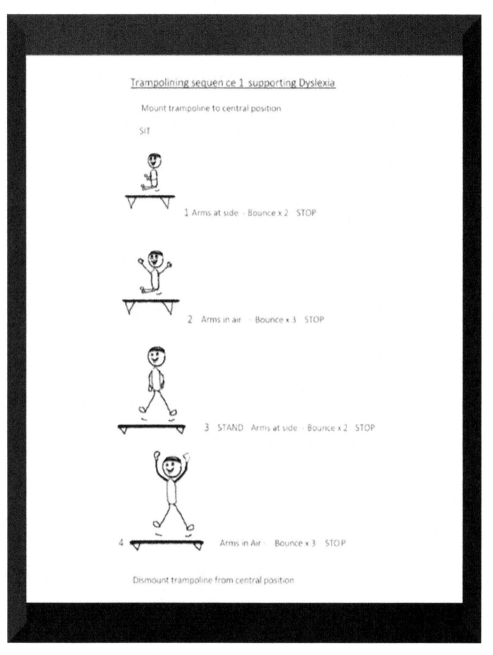

Figure 7.1 Trampoline Sequence 1 supporting Dyslexia

Trampolining sequencing 2

Mount trampoline to central position
Lie on back
Arms at side - Bounce x 2

Arms and legs in star shape - Bounce x 3

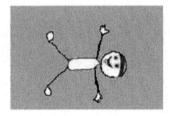

Get on hands and knees

Bounce x 5

Dismount trampoline from central position

Figure 7.2 Trampoline Sequence 2 supporting Dyslexia

Trampolining sequence 3 supporting Dyslexia

Mount trampoline to central position

1 Stand- Arms at side Bounce x 5 ▽ ▽ STOP

2 Arms down Knees up Bounce x 3 ▽ ▽ STOP

3 Arms up Knees up Bounce ▽ ▽ STOP

4 Arms out Legs out Star Jump ▽ ▽ STOP Dismount

Figure 7.3 Trampoline Sequence 3 supporting Dyslexia

Trampoline Sequence 4 supporting Dyslexia

Mount trampoline to central position

1 ⊽_____⊽ Arms up Bounce 5 times

2 ⊽_____ Throw bean bag counting out aloud in sequence

. Teacher will start numbers off. Student and teacher to take in turns counting on.

3 Free bouncing for 2 mins using sand timer

Dismount trampoline from central position

Figure 7.4 Trampoline Sequence 4 supporting Dyslexia

Trampoline Sequence 5 supporting Dyslexia

Mount trampoline to central position

1 Free bouncing to 1-minute sand timer

2 Throw ball to coach/teacher shouting out letter of alphabet

3 Catch ball as teacher shouts out next letter in sequence

4 Return ball to coach/teacher shouting out next letter in sequence. Continue for as long as possible

Dismount trampoline from central position

Figure 7.5 Trampoline Sequence 5 supporting Dyslexia

Trampolining sequencing

Mount trampoline to central position

Sit

Arms at side - Bounce x 2
Arms in air   - Bounce x 3

Stand

Arms at side - Bounce x 2
Arms in Air-   Bounce x 3

Dismount trampoline from central position

Figure 7.6 Trampoline Sequence 6 supporting Dyslexia

Resource 7.1 Word Art cards

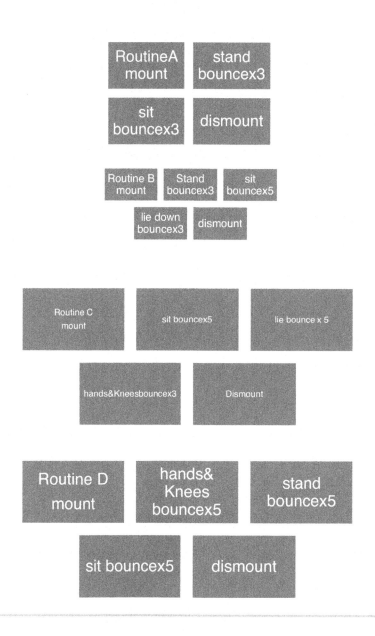

RoutineA mount

stand bouncex3

sit bouncex3

dismount

Routine B mount

Stand bouncex3

sit bouncex5

lie down bouncex3

dismount

Routine C mount

sit bouncex5

lie bounce x 5

hands&Kneesbouncex3

Dismount

Routine D mount

hands& Knees bouncex5

stand bouncex5

sit bouncex5

dismount

Resource 7.2 Template of leaflet advertising Trampoline Therapy (this leaflet can be folded)

Trampoline therapy sessions at ___ school

At . . . . . we promote a holistic approach to the education and support we offer every student attending our school. As part of this approach we are delighted that we can offer Trampoline and Rebound Therapy sessions as an addition to our extensive list of therapies.

Trampoline Therapy uses the moving surface of a trampoline to provide therapeutic exercise and recreation for people with a wide range of special needs.

Figure 7.7 Leaflet 1

The physiological benefits of Trampoline Therapy include improving:

- cardio-respiratory function,
- muscle tone,
- balance,
- spatial awareness.

Trampoline Therapy can also be used to strengthen limbs, stimulate communication including the use of Makaton signing and PECs, improve co-ordination, eye contact and turn-taking.

A variety of physiotherapy equipment is used in each session such as 'Nessie®' 'Peanuts', physiotherapy balls and bean bags.

Parachutes, ribbons, bubble wrap etc. are also employed to deliver a more sensory experience for the child.

If you would like further information, please take a look at our web page or contact us here at school on . . . . We will be delighted to answer any questions you may have.

Thank you.

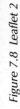

Figure 7.8 Leaflet 2

SCHOOL NAME:

Phone:

Resource 7.3 Contraindications leaflet

Precautions

If **any** of the following are present, **then your Therapist must be notified,** and special precautions must be taken.

TRAMPOLINE THERAPY CONTRAINDICATIONS

Cardiac or circulatory problems
Respiratory problems
Vertigo, blackouts or nausea
Epilepsy
Spinal cord or neck problems
Spinal rodding
Open wounds
Any recent medical attention
Brittle bones/osteoporosis
Friction effects on the skin (tender, fragile)
Unstable/hypermobile/painful joints
Hernia
Implant surgery (e.g. Baclofen pump)
Prolapse
Severe challenging behaviour
Gastrostomy/colostomy
Gastric reflux
Stress incontinence
Joint replacement/implant surgery
Haemophilia
Arthritis or Stills Disease
Muscular Dystrophy
Spina Bifida or Hydrocephalus
Changeable muscle tone
Dislocated hips/other joint problems
Tracheostomy

THE FOLLOWING ARE ABSOLUTE CONTRAINDICATIONS TO THERAPEUTIC TRAMPOLINING

Atlantoaxial instability
Detaching retina
Pregnancy

Table 7.1 Therapeutic Trampolining Screening Form

Name of student	
Date of birth	
Address	
Telephone number	
Name and telephone number of emergency contact	
Primary diagnosis	
Any other relevant factors	
Weight	
Height	

Please also complete overleaf. Thank You

Important

If you answer **YES** to any of the questions, please consult your GP to ask if they have any objection to your child receiving therapeutic trampolining and sign in the appropriate space below.

Please answer with as much detail as possible if you answer YES to any question.

Does the person named on the overleaf suffer from any of the following?

Condition	Yes	No
Circulatory disorders (high/low blood pressure, phlebitis, heart condition, etc)		
Spinal cord or neck problems		
Vertigo, blackouts, nausea		
Epilepsy		
Brittle bones		
Cancer/Neuritis/Multiple Sclerosis		
Skin disorder or infection		
Joint replacement		
Warts/Verruca's/splinters/bruises		
Arthritis		
Recent fractures, sprains or injuries		
Medication		
Any operations less than 6 months ago		

If you have answered YES to any of the questions above, please sign below to say you have obtained your GP's oral non-objection.

Signed: **Date:**

By signing this declaration, you agree to follow any protocols put in place for safety and have read and understood the Therapeutic Policy in place for our school.

SIGNED:	(parent/guardian of student)
PRINT NAME:	
DATE:	
***School use*: Received and assessed by:**	**Date:**

Table 7.2 Individual Session Recording

Name: Term: Class: Teacher: Therapist:

Target – <u>communicate wants more</u> Picture Evidence:	Target - Comments –
Comments –	Comments –
Comments –	Comments –

Evaluation	Any Suggestions

(RfL -Routes for Learning)

Table 7.3 Trampoline Therapy Session Sheet

Pupil: Date: Session Length: . . . .   Staff:

Target for session:
B Squared targets/RfL targets:
Responses
Wellbeing
Evaluation. Was the session successful/unsuccessful? If so, why?
Any suggestions that may help in future sessions?

eRESOURCES

Table 7.4 Scheme of Work – Trampolining for Students with Additional Learning Needs (ALN)

Subject: Trampolining	Following British Gymnastics level 1 Award	DURATION: 6 LESSONS
AIM: In this unit students will focus on the basic safety issues around the trampoline. Students will learn the rules of the trampoline. They will observe trampoline demonstrations by those used to following the rules and the basic safety requirements. Students will learn individual trampoline skills and a sequence of skills. They will learn to develop turn-taking, patience and following instructions. The students will follow the BG Trampoline Proficiency Award scheme beginning at Badge 1. Depending on whether the student can stand, they may be taught to stand and bounce. If the student is unable to stand, they may be taught to sit and bounce.		
PRIOR LEARNING It is helpful if the students have: • Experienced some of the safety aspects. • Experienced the getting out and putting away of the equipment e.g. balls, bean bags. • Experienced turn-taking. • Experienced basic jumping and stopping.	LITERACY NUMERACY/PSHE Through the activities in this unit students will be able to understand the meanings of the basic words used, to take turns, communicate their understanding of directions and develop their listening skills. They will be able to count or correctly respond to the number of bounces asked for.	RESOURCES • Trampolines • Gymnastics mats • Safety crash mats • Routine cards • Nessie®
Key Concepts and Processes		
Accurate Replication Students should be able to accurately replicate basic movements. Students will be able to demonstrate correct take-off and landing technique, as well as a clear body shape.	**Developing Physical and Mental Capacity** Students will understand the importance of safety requirements and understand the basics of landing properly. Students will learn the basic principle of routines when compiling a sequence *i.e. 3 bounces and what constitutes 1 bounce.*	**Developing Skills/Performance** Throughout this scheme students will develop the skills necessary to develop sequence routines. They will learn to move around the trampoline bed. They will learn to sit and bounce/rock. They will learn to stand and bounce/rock. They will learn to lie on their backs and bounce. They will learn to do hands and knees bounces.

Making and Applying Decisions	Making Informed Choices About Healthy, Active Lifestyles	Evaluating and Improving
Students will develop and refine skills into a simple sequenced routine. Students will follow Trampoline Rules and learn to stop when asked. They will mount and dismount correctly.	Students will understand how performance and safety are improved when preparation is carried out properly and rules are followed.	Students will be able to observe and improve the performance of self and others through peer observation and assessment.

Cross-Curricular Links: Literacy (key words), listening, PSHE (turn-taking and cooperation), numeracy (counting)

Assessment: Q & A, Formative and Summative Assessment

Extension and Enrichment

Out of lessons, at home and in the community, students could be encouraged to:

- join school or local trampolining clubs.
- organise trampolining displays or competitions for students to take part in and watch.
- watch trampolining live or on video.

Language for learning

Through the activities in this unit students will be able to understand and use words relating to trampoline safety and rules to remember.

Speaking and listening – through the activities students could:

- discuss and respond to why rules are important and how to keep safe while trampolining.

Expectations

After carrying out the activities and core tasks in this unit,

most students will: land safely on the trampoline; select and apply learned techniques and demonstrate control of their body when performing these; link movements effectively and so develop a sequence; identify and work on the skills taught.

some students will not have made so much progress and will: perform simple skills with reasonable control; move into and out of individual actions with guidance.

some students will have progressed further and will: understand all the trampoline rules and follow them, complete level 1 with ease showing confidence on the trampoline.

By the end of this unit a pupil will reach level 1 by being able to:

Aid in the finding and returning of simple equipment. Understand why people 'spot' correctly and safely. Accurately replicate basic moves and routines from the level 1 BG Proficiency Award with some control. Combine moves into a short sequence. Display some understanding of the terminology used.

Table 7.5 Trampoline Lesson Plans for Students with ALN

WEEK	LEARNING OBJECTIVES	TASK EXAMPLES	POINTS TO NOTE/ DIFFERENTIATION
1	**Lesson 1** To understand the rules needed for trampolining. To be able to move around the trampoline bed. To land safely from a jump. Learn to jump/ bounce up and down with total control. To accurately replicate basic sit/stand bounces with good body tension and posture. To develop students turn-taking and safety awareness.	Intro health and safety aspects, spotting role, 1 on at a time. Go through trampoline rules and why they are necessary. Demonstrate how to mount and dismount, get around trampoline bed; when you land, all you need is a slight bend in the knee. Too much bend absorbs all the power and you will stop bouncing; how to sit and bounce, stand and bounce. Emphasis on control. Teaching points; sitting with support of adult/ control without support/using equipment e.g. Nessie®. Sitting bouncing. Standing with support of adult/without support. Standing bouncing with support/without support. Learning to STOP. Dismount safely.	Engage students in learning through physical activity. Provide opportunities to watch others, perform, demonstrate + coach. Give the students the opportunity to communicate with each other.
2	**Lesson 2** To revise the rules needed for trampolining. To accurately replicate basic sit/stand rocking movements and bounces with good body tension and posture. To continue to develop students turn-taking and safety awareness	Intro health and safety aspects. Go through trampoline rules and why they are necessary. Demonstration: how to get around trampoline bed, how to sit and rock, stand and rock. Emphasis on control. Teaching points; sitting with support of adult/without support/using equipment e.g. Nessie®. Sitting rocking. Standing with support of adult/without support. Standing rocking with support/without support. Learning to STOP. Dismount safely.	Use video to record performance. Develop knowledge of appropriate progressions in order to coach others.
3	**Lesson 3** To revise the rules needed for trampolining. To accurately replicate basic lying down on back bounces with good body tension and posture. To continue to develop students turn-taking and safety awareness.	Intro health and safety aspects. Go through trampoline rules and why they are necessary. Demonstration: how to sit and rock, stand and rock; how to lie down on trampoline and bounce. Emphasis on control. Teaching points; support of adult to show how to lie on back on trampoline/without support/lying bouncing, making shapes while lying on back with support of adult/ without support. Learning to STOP. Dismount safely.	

4	**Lesson 4** To revise the rules needed for trampolining. To accurately replicate basic hands and knees bounces with good body tension and posture. To continue to develop students turn-taking and safety awareness.	Intro health and safety aspects, go through trampoline rules and why they are necessary. Demonstration: how to get on hands and knees on trampoline and bounce. Emphasis on control. Teaching points; support of adult to show how to get on hands and knees on trampoline/without support/hands and knees bouncing, with support of adult/without support. Learning to STOP. Dismount safely.
5	**Lesson 5** To revise the rules needed for trampolining. To accurately replicate sequences learnt with good body tension and posture to continue to develop students turn-taking and safety awareness.	Recap prior learning. Demonstration combination of learned routines: sit, bounce, rock, stand, bounce, rock, lie on back bounce, hands and knees bounce. Teaching points: support student to copy the combination of routines stopping correctly before moving on. Dismount correctly.
6	**Routines + Assessment** To accurately replicate learnt skills and to create simple routines for assessment. To improve students' appreciation of performance and evaluate ways of improving.	Recap learnt skills. Develop sequence. Can use cards as guideline. Peer assessment – level each performance. Teacher grades against BG level 1.

Table 7.6 Scheme of Work – Trampolining for Students with Profound and Multiple Learning Difficulties (PMLD)

Subject: Trampolining	Following Winstrada level 1 Rebound Therapy	DURATION: 6 LESSONS
AIM: In this unit students and teaching assistant accompanying them will be introduced on the basic safety issues around the trampoline and the trampoline rules (displayed on the wall) and a sequence of skills. They will learn to develop turn-taking, patience and following instructions. The students will follow the Winstrada Trampoline Proficiency Award scheme beginning at level 1.		
PRIOR LEARNING It is helpful if the students have: ● Experienced being hoisted. ● Experienced turn-taking. ● Experienced basic stopping of a task.	LITERACY NUMERACY/PSHE Students will learn to take turns; follow directions and develop their listening skills. They will be able to respond to communicating their desire for 'more'. They will increase body awareness.	RESOURCES ○ Trampolines ○ Gymnastics mats ○ Safety crash mats ○ Nessie®-trampoline sitting aid ○ Communication aid ○ Music
Key Concepts and Processes:		
Accurate Replication Students will learn to show and hold star position lying on trampoline; to sit and bounce with support; to stand and bounce with support.	**Developing Physical and Mental Capacity** Students will be shown the importance of safety requirements. They will develop physical strength and stamina. They will respond with body and mind to trampoline movement and learn to relax. They will improve their balance. Students show enjoyment. They will learn to weight bear with support and develop head control.	**Developing Skills/Performance** Students will be hoisted onto the trampoline/or assisted up the steps. They will be monitored to assess whether they develop confidence in this method of mounting the trampoline. Students will be changed into appropriate clothing for the session and monitored to assess whether they indicate that they know where they are going and whether they assist in the changing. They will be assessed once on the trampoline regarding their communication e.g. using their method of communication to ask for 'more' bounces. They will be assessed on trampoline skills using the Winstrada Proficiency Grade 1.

Making and Applying Decisions
Students will develop and refine skills so that they can follow directions on the trampoline.
Students will follow Trampoline Rules and learn to stop when asked. They will mount and dismount correctly with support.

Cross-Curricular Links: Literacy (key words), listening, PSHE (turn-taking and cooperation), numeracy (responding to counting)

Extension and Enrichment
Out of lessons, at home and in the community, students could be encouraged to:

• join school or local trampolining clubs supporting students with PMLD.

Language for learning
Through the activities in this unit students will be able to understand words/signs relating to requesting more, being asked to STOP. Lesson is finished.
Speaking and listening/signing/gesture – through the activities students could maintain eye contact for a few seconds, sign/ask for 'more'.

Making Informed Choices About Healthy, Active Lifestyles
Students will increase body awareness, spatial awareness, proprioception and sensory awareness.

Assessment: Q & A, Formative and Summative Assessment

Expectations
After carrying out the activities and core tasks in this unit, most students will: show enjoyment on the trampoline; anticipate cause and effect; differentiate between stillness and movement; regain position when moved off balance; bounce and stop bouncing.

some students will not have made so much progress and will: perform simple skills with reasonable control; move into and out of individual actions with guidance.

some students will have progressed further and will: understand all the trampoline rules and follow them, complete a section or chosen numbers of sections of Grade 1, showing enjoyment on the trampoline.

Evaluating and Improving
Students will be able to observe and improve their performance. They will be able to perform peer observation and assessment.

By the end of this unit a pupil will reach completion of some of the 28 movements of Grade 1 by:

Accurately replicating basic moves and those from Grade 1 with some control. Displaying some understanding of the terminology used.

Table 7.7 Trampoline Lesson Plans for Students with PMLD

	LEARNING OBJECTIVES	TASK EXAMPLES	POINTS TO NOTE/ DIFFERENTIATION
1	**Lesson 1** To be able to mount/dismount the trampoline via a hoist or supported up/down steps. To lie or stand on trampoline supported and feel the movement of the trampoline as it is bounced by coach. To develop students turn-taking and safety awareness.	Teaching points; hoisting – fears of being out of control as lifted – encouragement, talk student through process, ask student to help with putting arms through sling etc with support of adult. Gentle release of hoist to trampoline bed. Removal of sling with care. Gentle movement of trampoline by adult for student to experience what being on a trampoline means. Walking up steps – support student to encourage stepping onto an unsteady surface and maintaining balance with support/ without support. Encourage ambulant person to walk around trampoline. Encourage non-ambulant person to move around trampoline to feel sensation and maintain balance.	Engage students in learning through physical activity. Provide opportunities to watch others, perform, demonstrate + coach. Give the students the opportunity to communicate with each other. Use video to record performance.
2	**Lesson 2** To revise the mounting and dismounting procedures. To accurately replicate moving around trampoline. To lie or stand and experience bouncing with good body tension and posture. To continue to develop students turn-taking and safety awareness.	Go through relevant trampoline rules and why they are necessary. Demonstration: Revision on how to get around trampoline bed, how to lie/stand and bounce. Emphasis on control. Teaching points; lie/stand with support of adult/without support. Learning to STOP. Dismount safely. Learning to communicate the desire for 'more' bounces.	Develop knowledge of appropriate progressions in order to coach others.

3	**Lesson 3** To revise the mounting/dismounting procedures. To accurately replicate basic lying down on back/standing bounces with good body tension and posture. To continue to develop students turn-taking and safety awareness.	Go through relevant trampoline rules and why they are necessary. Demonstration: how to lie and rock, stand and rock; how to lie down on trampoline and bounce. Emphasis on control. Teaching points; support of adult to show how to lie on back on trampoline/without support/lying bouncing, making shapes while lying on back with support of adult/without support. Learning to regain position when moved off balance. Learning to STOP. Dismount safely.	
4	**Lesson 4** To revise the mounting dismounting procedures. To accurately replicate a set number of bounces. To request more bounces when bounces have stopped. To continue to develop students turn-taking and safety awareness.	Go through relevant trampoline rules and why they are necessary. Demonstration: Count 3 bounces and stop. Say/sign/show PECs symbol/use Big Mac to demonstrate request for 'more' then count 3 bounces and stop. Repeat as necessary. Emphasis on control. Teaching points: Using communication aid to ask for more. Recognising of 3 separate bounces. Learning to STOP. Dismount safely.	
5	**Lesson 5** To revise the mounting dismounting procedures. To accurately replicate basic sit/stand bounces with good body tension and posture to develop students turn-taking and safety awareness.	Go through relevant trampoline rules and why they are necessary. Demonstrate how to sit and bounce, stand and bounce; Emphasis on control. Teaching points; sitting with support of adult/without support/using equipment e.g. Nessie®. Sitting bouncing. Standing with support of adult/without support. Standing bouncing with support/without support. Learning to STOP. Dismount safely.	
6	**Lesson 6** To revise the mounting dismounting procedures. To accurately replicate learnt skills for assessment. To develop students turn-taking and safety awareness.	Recap learnt skills. Teacher grades against Winstrada Grade 1.	

Table 7.8 Communication Placemat

Communication	Independence	How I show my feelings
	-- **Diagnosis** **Medication** **Allergies** **D.O.B**.	
Things I like		**Things I don't like**
Curriculum	**Food and Drink** **Special People** **Out and about**	**REMEMBER**

These cards can be cut out and handed to students as a visual reminder

Figure 7.9 Mini Trampoline Programme

Table 7.9 Individual Education Plan (IEP)

Name: **Term:**

Class: **Teacher:**

English	
. . . . will recognise rhyme through verse (Writing 1C)	
Maths	
. . . . will sort shapes by size (SSM L1C)	
PSHE	
. . . . will discuss with the teacher what he requires for an activity (PSHE L1C)	
Computing	
. . . . will know there are different types of content on a website (L1)	
Literacy and Numeracy Framework	
Literacy . . . . will use capital letters and full stops with some degree of consistency (Y1) *Numeracy* . . . . will use the concept of time in terms of their daily and weekly activities and the seasons of the year (Y1) *Digital Competence* . . . . will sort given pictures (e.g. insects) and words into groups, using one or more criteria, giving reasons for their grouping (Y1)	

Pupil uses a TEACCH® Station | Y |

Pupil has an Individual Behaviour Plan | Y |

Note: The attainment levels used for children in Wales are P1–8 (working towards National Curriculum Level 1) and NC1–8 (Levels covering ages 3–16, each Level is divided into A–C, where A is upper, C is lower). On average the majority of children in Wales achieve a Level 2B by the time they finish Foundation Phase, and Level 4B by the end of their primary education. Information about the curriculum in Wales, including Levels, can be found at http://learning.gov.wales

Resource 7.4 Sensory, Therapeutic & Physical Wellbeing Policy

Areas of Learning and Experience (AoLE)

Introduction

This policy explains the nature of Sensory, Therapeutic & Physical Wellbeing policy within the school and its contribution to the education of students at this Special School.

Aims

Sensory, Therapeutic & Physical Wellbeing policy offers students the opportunity:

- To promote positive health (mental and physical) wellbeing
- To work independently and collaboratively whilst developing their personal communication skills
- To develop self-awareness, confidence and self-esteem
- To meet students' individual sensory, therapeutic and physical needs
- To encourage choice-making skills through a range of activities and approaches
- To promote a love for outdoor and community learning

Four purposes

We follow the guidance of the 'Successful Futures' Curriculum for the Welsh Assembly Governments pioneering curriculum and professional learning work. We endorse the aims of The National Curriculum to provide a broad and balanced curriculum.

Sensory, Therapeutic & Physical Wellbeing policy endorses the four purposes and believe that all our children at this school will be:

- Ambitious, capable learners who are ready to learn throughout their lives.
- Enterprising, creative contributors who are ready to play a full part in life and work.
- Ethical, informed citizens who are ready to be citizens of Wales and the world.
- Healthy, confident individuals who have the skills and knowledge to manage everyday life as independently as they can and are ready to lead fulfilling lives as valued members of society.

Content

It encompasses traditional PE, gross motor skills development and therapeutic approaches to movement including individual physiotherapy programmes. We

(Continued)

(*Continued*)

endeavour to tailor the curriculum to meet students' individual sensory, therapeutic and physical needs. We want our children to experience a range of activities and approaches.

Sensory, Therapeutic & Physical Wellbeing policy offers a range of activities and experiences which are rotated throughout the year. The activities and experiences offered may include:

- Hydrotherapy
- Trampoline
- Sherborne
- Swimming
- RDA
- Sensory Circuits
- Cosmic Yoga
- Outdoor Play
- Soft Play
- Athletics
- Games
- Cheerleading and Community events including dance and performance, Special Sports including Panathlon and Boccia.

Planning

At this school we follow a rolling programme of topics in a 3-year cycle in the Foundation department and in a 4-year cycle in the Key Stage Two department. Teachers are responsible for providing 6 medium term plans in Foundation department and 4 in key stage (which includes Sensory, Therapeutic & Physical Wellbeing policy medium term planning). In Nursery and Foundation departments, this is included across Health and Wellbeing planning.

Teachers are responsible for providing weekly planning for staff to see in their classes as well as a class weekly timetable outside on the class door.

Teachers set different tasks during Sensory, Therapeutic & Physical Wellbeing policy to meet the specific needs of their class as well as individual students. Teachers ensure that activities and therapies are fairly distributed throughout the school year to ensure students experience a broad and balanced curriculum.

Equal opportunities

Sensory, Therapeutic & Physical Wellbeing policy is delivered to all students regardless of gender, culture or ability.

Special needs

All teachers must make themselves aware of any relevant medical needs or learning difficulty, which may affect a student's ability to learn. The activity ideas are in the form of topic-based planning and can be adapted to suit students by referring to the PMLD and Alternative Curriculum materials.

I.C.T.

Students use a variety of computer programs and iPad Apps for Sensory, Therapeutic & Physical Wellbeing. Student work may be recorded using an iPad.

Assessment, recording and reporting of student progress

Evaluation of learning outcomes comes from the Sensory, Therapeutic & Physical Wellbeing Skills Ladder based on B Squared. This covers PE and PSHE and will inform future planning. Students with PMLD learning outcomes will continue to come from the Routes for Learning assessment and will inform future planning. A summary of work covered, and progress made is given in the end of year summer report for Nursery, Foundation and Key Stage Two.

Monitoring and evaluation of Sensory, Therapeutic & Physical Wellbeing policy

The Sensory, Therapeutic & Physical Wellbeing policy AoLE group carry out a detailed Monitoring and Evaluation report. As part of this process the AoLE group looks at all aspects of how Sensory, Therapeutic and Physical Wellbeing support is delivered in school and its relationship to student progress, including resources. An action plan for further development is then drawn up. Monitoring and Evaluation is carried out on a rolling programme every 2 years.

Health and safety

All staff must have due regard to the health and safety of their students during Sensory, Therapeutic and Physical Wellbeing sessions when different materials are being used.
   Students should be taught to:

* Consider and follow simple rules that help them keep safe.
* Consider how to reduce the risk by changing the situation or the way they behave.

Review

This policy will be reviewed regularly.

Resource 7.5 Therapeutic Trampolining Policy

This policy explains the nature of Trampolining within the school and its contribution to the education of students at . . . . School.

This policy has been shared and approved by the teaching staff and school governors.

Aims

Trampolining offers students the opportunity to develop and improve:

- Strength of limbs
- Numeracy
- Patience
- Communication
- Co-ordination
- Independence
- Self-confidence
- Balance
- Muscle tone
- Reaction speed
- Self-image
- Eye contact

- Relaxation
- Freedom of movement
- Sense of achievement
- Stamina
- Spatial awareness
- Body awareness
- Social awareness
- Consideration of others
- Trust and confidence in Coach/Assistant
- Colour recognition
- Height and depth perception
- Fun and enjoyment

Rebound Therapy may also offer students the benefits of

- Stimulation of digestive system
- Improved bowel function
- Internal organ massage
- Clearing of toxins from the body

Trampolining should be a personal and pleasurable experience, which enriches the lives of the students. Students will follow either the British Gymnastics (BG) Programme or the Winstrada Programme depending on assessment by coach. Students may follow independent physiotherapy programmes, curricular extension programmes, Sensory programmes or Rebound Therapy programmes.

The phrase 'Rebound Therapy' was coined by the founder, E.G. Anderson, in 1969 to describe the use of trampolines in providing therapeutic exercise and recreation for people with a wide range of special needs.

Rebound Therapy is used to facilitate movement, promote balance, promote an increase or decrease in muscle tone, promote relaxation, promote sensory integration, improve fitness and exercise tolerance, and to improve communication skills.

Entitlement

We endorse the aims of the Curriculum to provide a broad and balanced curriculum and deliver trampolining to enable students to access an appropriate curriculum.

Planning

Teachers match educational targets, where possible using B Squared and/or Routes for Learning (RfL). They share and discuss those targets with the Trampoline Coach who has been trained in Rebound Therapy. The coach and the teacher may also choose targets which support the well-being of the student. Teachers set different targets to meet the specific needs of individual students.

Figure 7.10   *Figure 7.11*

Therapies and physical development and physical education

At our school we promote a holistic approach to the education and support we offer every student attending our school. We have an extensive list of therapies that enhance the delivery of a broad and balanced curriculum for the physical development of our students. The following therapies below support and enhance the Physical Development and Physical Education in the national curriculum at our School.

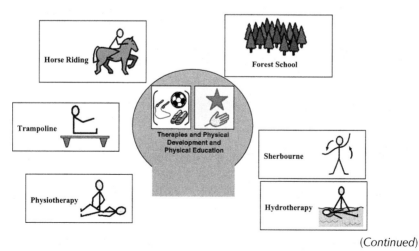

(Continued)

(*Continued*)

Equal opportunities

Trampolining is delivered to students regardless of gender, culture or ability. Boys and girls have equal access to this therapy.

Resources

Trampolining is delivered in a trampoline room. The trampoline is standing. Two people are present when delivering sessions. A hoist is used for some students though steps up to the trampoline are also in situ.

Assessment, recording and reporting of student progress

Evaluation of learning outcomes comes from individual B Squared planning and/or RfL. This evaluation is used to inform future planning. An assistant records the progress made by students towards their targets after each session on the Winstrada forms/ BG forms/Sensory forms and records any evidence that the therapy has supported the well-being of the student on forms produced by the school. These recording sheets are copied and placed in an individual's class file. Teachers use this evidence to write end of session reports home to inform parents of the progress made by their child and write reports for each student's annual review. An evaluation sheet is completed by the class teacher to show the impact of the therapy on the students learning and/or health.

Monitoring and evaluation of trampolining

The Therapies Consultant carries out detailed monitoring and evaluation of Trampoline Therapy. As part of the process the consultant looks at all aspects of how Trampoline Therapy is delivered in school and its relationship to student progress. An action plan for further development is then drawn up. Monitoring and evaluation are carried out on a rolling programme every two years.

Supervision

The trampoline coach and PE consultant have overall responsibility for the supervision and general safety of all those receiving the therapeutic session. They will evaluate every application to assess the student's suitability to receive trampolining.

Data handling

It is essential that there are maintained, appropriate and detailed records. The school must ensure they are kept confidentially and adhere to data protection legislation ensuring all records held are appropriate and stored securely.

Health and hygiene

The trampoline coach must ensure they maintain a safe environment for their students. The trampoline room should be warm, clean, and comfortable and be free from all potential hazards.

Risk assessments

A risk assessment should be carried out in respect of each student referred for trampolining. This will include any mobility issues that may require the use of the hoist and an individual manual handling plan will be put in place if necessary. If a student has a medical condition that requires constant monitoring it may be deemed necessary for an additional member of staff to accompany the student to ensure their individual health needs are being met. A risk assessment has been completed for the use of the trampoline in the room.

Accident procedures

All accidents or incidents that occur whilst in the trampoline room or on the way to or from the room must be immediately reported to the Head Teacher and guidance sought from a qualified first aider if appropriate. An accident form should be obtained from the school office and completed timeously (within 24 hours of the incident/accident).

Other guidance

It is appreciated that whilst every care may be taken to promote safety, there may be occasions and situations that occur despite safety precautions being in place. In such an eventuality further clarification and advice will be sought from the Head Teacher who may seek further guidance from the local authority.

8 | Trampolining at home

Figure 8.1 Bouncy castle

Even as babies and toddlers we love to bounce, whether it's in a baby bouncer or on a bouncy castle.

In today's technological age it can be difficult encouraging our children to exercise. Children don't seem to see bouncing on their beds or the sofa as exercising but as having fun. Luckily, they see trampolining in the same way. Yet trampolining is such a powerful exercise that it can aid the development of a strong skeletal system due to the repetitive impact of jumping on a rebounding surface. Jumping up and down repeatedly on a concrete floor would not do the skeletal system any good and it would not be as much fun.

There are many different rebounders available. Rebounders are trampolines that are smaller in size and so are also known as mini trampolines. Some of them have handrails to aid stability. These are ideal for indoors and can give relief to a child with autism before feelings of stress leads to a complete meltdown. They are well worth purchasing but a parent would need to do their research to ensure that it was a sturdy model with a good bounce and that it was safe to use. They tend not to be recommended for children under the age of six but there is such a thing as a

Jump-O-Lene available which looks like a small child's version of a mini trampoline and is virtually an inflatable bouncer with reinforced net sidewalls providing a safe enclosed play area. It is available from special needs catalogues, but you can also find it cheaper online if you just Google its name. It has high walls to ensure safety.

It provides, as does a mini trampoline, vestibular stimulation to the user. It will help your child develop motor skills, giving them more strength and control of their body and muscles. It is suitable for ages 3–6. It is 72 × 208cm in diameter.

There are a lot of schools and clubs using mini trampolines now as a high-energy activity or as part of a sensory circuit. Parents can either let their child follow a DVD workout that often comes with the rebounder, let their child just bounce at their own pace, or ask their child's school for guidance. There is guidance in using trampolines and mini trampolines in this book in chapter 7 and on risks and rules in chapter 9. There are also videos on YouTube that they can follow.

Most mini trampolines can be folded flat for easy storage but if your child is someone who needs to use it as and when they begin to feel stressed, then it is probably best to designate an area in the home for it. Rebounders typically range from 107cm to 122cm in diameter and are circular. They usually come with a detachable handrail and these need to be attached if your child needs that support. It must be your decision whether they need the handrail and not theirs.

I have a mini trampoline that folds in half and has its own storage bag but my grandchildren use it several times a day and so it has never been inside the bag. However, if I needed to take it away with us if we were to go on holiday in this country, then I could easily take it with me. Mini trampolines are a fantastic form of exercise, whatever the persons age, and can improve the ability to regain balance in the elderly (Aragao et al. 2016). Modified trampoline training has also been proven to significantly improve balance, dynamic gait, and falls efficacy of stroke patients. Suggesting that modified mini trampoline training is a feasible and effective way of improving balance, dynamic gait, and falls efficacy after stroke (Hahn et al. 2015).

When using a mini trampoline ordinary play clothes or sports clothes can be worn but it is preferable to be barefoot because you would lose part of the benefits of rebounding if you wore footwear. This is different to a full-sized trampoline when it is best to wear socks or trampoline footwear.

Outdoor trampolines

Safety guidelines from RoSPA state that trampolining isn't suitable for children under the age of six as they are unable to control their bouncing.

You will need to have your garden's measurements before purchasing an outdoor trampoline. Outdoor trampolines that reach recognised safety standards can be expensive. The most popular ones until 2019 are like the one in Figure 8.2 that has a UV-resistant netting. The safety netting reduces the risk of your child falling off the trampoline and hitting the solid ground. Large outdoor trampolines should be in a clear space so that there are no overhanging branches or washing lines to get caught on, no glass greenhouses to fall onto etc. It all sounds like common sense but often in the excitement and rush to put up the trampoline, these things get overlooked – until it is too late.

Figure 8.2 Garden trampoline with netting

As you can see from the picture trampolines often come with a ladder provided that must be aligned with the net entrance so that children can get immediately into a netted environment. The one in the picture is also galvanised and galvanised frames and springs minimise the possibility of rust. When you consider that your trampoline will be out in all weathers then galvanised frames and springs make sense. A sturdy base is important as the last thing you want is for the trampoline to tip over whilst your child was jumping on it. A trampoline with a weighted base or one that can be secured to the ground should be your first choice. Otherwise you will need to purchase anchors yourself and secure it.

Check that any padding is of good quality so that it will last. It may be the slightly dearer trampoline, but it will save you paying for replacement padding in the long term. You will need to check that the padding covers the powerful metal springs that attach the jumping bed to its frame. Trampolines are a long-term investment so make sure that you have a warranty. Some warranties can be for up to 10 years. Reputable manufacturers often extend their warranties for free.

Nowadays there are trampolines that can be purchased with extra features such as a detachable basketball hoop and LED lights so that it can be used in the night-time.

In 2019 in-ground garden trampolines became popular. Embedded in the ground they meet European safety standards with no need for safety nets. Some children enjoy walking around the outside of the safety net on the frame of the free-standing trampoline and if you feel your child may be inclined to do that than an in-ground trampoline may be the safer option.

All home trampolines are only designed to be used by one person at a time. Please see the Garden Trampoline Safety document from the British Gymnastics (BG) website written in 2009 at: www.british-gymnastics.org/documents/departments/membership/health-safety/1591-garden-trampoline-safety-statement/file

RoSPA has more up-to-date guidance, written in 2015. It is called the Garden Trampoline Briefing Paper and is available at www.rospa.com

When BG wrote its guidance in 2009, garden trampolines were not as popular as they are today. RoSPA claims that trampoline manufacturers estimate that they sold between 200.000 to 250.000 in the UK in 2014.

Guidance in both documents suggest that the biggest cause of injuries on a garden trampoline is caused by more than one person bouncing on the trampoline at the same time, even though guidelines warn you against this. I have watched children on garden trampolines, and I think it is because they all want to be on it, and no one is prepared to wait and take turns, and no one is regularly supervising them. When RoSPA investigated trampoline injuries, it was telling to note that accidents in a regulated and controlled environment such as a club or school were rare.

Six easy-to-remember rules for children (aged 6 and over) using the garden trampoline

1   Only one person on the trampoline at any time.
2   Children should be told to bounce in the centre of the trampoline.
3   Jumping off the trampoline should be forbidden.
4   Trampoline skills should be taught properly before they can be used.
5   Always follow the manufacturer's instructions.
6   Always use a safety net.

The British Red Cross provides guidance on how to deal with common injuries and there is a free app that you can download from their website at www.redcross.org.uk

In the meantime, here is a precis of some basic advice that it gives in relation to trampoline-related accidents:

- If your child has received a bump to the head the advice is to ask them to rest and apply a cold compress to the injury. If they become drowsy or vomit, then call an ambulance or go immediately to A&E.
- If you believe your child has sprained or strained themselves – ask your child to rest while you apply an ice pack. If they don't improve after 10 minutes call an ambulance or take them to A&E.
- If you think your child may have a broken bone, is in pain and has bruising or swelling or the limb is at an odd angle, support the injury with a cushion to keep it still. Have someone support the injury while you call for an ambulance or take them to A&E.
- If your child sustains a nose-bleed get your child to pinch the soft part of their nose and lean forward, preferably for 10 minutes. This helps the blood to form a clot while stopping them swallowing blood.

Here are some links for ideas for things to do on your home trampoline:

www.youtube.com/watch?v=eCZ09EKFdSA
www.youtube.com/watch?v=cN_jplXveul
www.youtube.com/watch?v=PRO_IIRpe3o

Trampolining health and safety, rules and risk assessment

Trampolining is a very popular activity nowadays. They are used in schools, local clubs, leisure centres, parks and at home.

If you work in a school or college then you will need to produce consent forms so that parents give permission for their child to attend trampoline sessions. If you own a club or manage a trampoline park, then I humbly suggest that you do the same to protect your business from any legal claims against it. Please see chapter 7 for forms that I devised several years ago that are still in use at that school and now in several other schools too.

If a child has any illness or disability, then they will need to check with their GP or paediatrician to ensure it is safe for their child to go on a trampoline. If consent is given but with restrictions, then these will need to be shared by the class teacher with the trampoline coach or therapist. It is possibly a good idea to add it to the child's communication placemat or individual education plan to ensure that everyone is aware. A copy of a communication placemat and IEP can be found in chapter 7.

The British Gymnastics organisation produces a guidelines document that it updates regularly on Atlanto-Axial screening. Persons with Down Syndrome can suffer with this and if they wish to participate in any gymnastic activity, including trampolining then they will need to be screened. It is an excellent document and can be easily downloaded to be kept for reference from www.british-gymnastics.org/technical-information/discipline-updates/disabilities/9316-atlanto-axial-information-pack-1/file

An adapted copy of this document is available to copy towards the end of this chapter.

As health and safety is a huge concern with trampolining, it would make sense for schools and colleges to have a specific area in the trampoline room dedicated to health and safety rules agreed by the coach/therapist and senior management. If you were to ask a child what the priority of a trampoline was, they would probably say its bouncing ability. If you were to ask the coach or therapist, they would probably say the safety element. Please see chapter 7 for photocopiable materials and please feel free to download and print out the free documents that you may also wish to put on display. A photocopiable poster (including symbols) can be found towards the end of this chapter.

It has been great to have enthusiastic trampoline therapists who like to own the display boards in the trampoline room, and school inspectors have always been impressed with the advice on display.

If the trampoline is a free-standing trampoline, then you will need more than one person with the student. Depending on the size of the trampoline and whether the student is ambulant, you could need spotters. Spotters are members of staff who stand at the sides of the trampoline to offer support to trampolinists who may fall from the trampoline. This is particularly necessary if you are using a school or college hall and there is a lot of room around the trampoline. When I delivered trampolining to secondary special school students in such a hall, we had to have a spotter at each side of the trampoline. The students were often very large, some had balance difficulties and it was vital that we had spotters. On a trampoline it is quite easy to misstep when trying to walk or to sway excessively. Students with learning difficulties are particularly prone to balance issues because their cognition and coordination are often affected by their condition.

It is important that whatever we are doing on the trampoline with a student is explained at their cognitive level using whatever communication aid they are comfortable with. It is not just a fun activity. You are expecting something from the student. The student must process a lot of new information. This can take time and you need to allow for that time so that accidents don't happen. Take your time.

Proprioception gives us a sense of where our limbs are in relation to each other and what they are doing. Students with additional learning needs often have proprioception difficulties. They may have difficulty walking but this should not stop them accessing the trampoline if their difficulties are highlighted and taken into account.

Vision helps us to process information from all our senses as well as allowing us to see where we are and where to put our feet. A room that is used just for the trampoline must have plenty of light so that students can see to the best of their ability.

I have also noticed that students with a hearing loss can have difficulty with balance and gait.

The vestibular system is made up of tiny semi-circular canals of fluid in the inner ear. It allows us to detect movement in three dimensions. It is much like the body's own spirit level in that it enables us to maintain balance. Students with mobility problems may have a damaged vestibular system. This makes tripping and falling more likely.

When schools are considering getting a trampoline, the expense of the number of staff involved is one of the reasons why they choose not to.

Hippocrates, in his treatise on head injuries (400 BC), the first medical writing on falls, observed 'he who falls from a very high place upon a hard and blunt object is in most danger of sustaining a fracture . . . whereas he that falls upon level ground, upon a softer object, is likely to suffer less injury'. It therefore makes sense to have trampoline crash mats surrounding the trampoline as well as to cushion any fall. These mats must be secure so that students do not trip over any curled-up edges. Get rid of any mats that could pose a risk.

If you have steps leading up to the trampoline, then make rules for students using those steps. They should always hold the handrail. It is too easy for a student to fall forward and damage their teeth due to the excitement of wanting to get onto the trampoline quickly.

If a student is recovering from a recent seizure, then their session on the trampoline will need to be cancelled. There is a well-known phrase in sport now. It is 'If in doubt sit them out'. This is a phrase that should be taken on by anyone using the trampoline with students and regardless of whether they are delivering it as a therapy or as a sport.

The ideal place for a large trampoline in a school is to have it embedded in the floor surrounded by impact-absorbing flooring. I have worked in schools where the trampoline is portable and put up when required. This usually takes at least three people. I have trapped my fingers in the hinges of the trampoline, and it is very painful. I have heard of staff mysteriously disappearing when it is time to get the trampoline out. If it can be set up and left in a designated room or space, then staff injuries are less likely to occur. All trampolines must be regularly inspected and maintained. There is currently no British safety standard for school trampolines but there is one for domestic trampolines.

If your school does decide to have a trampoline installed in the ground, then it is a big deal. I had been at a previous school where the trampoline was embedded in the school hall with a wooden floor that slid over it. It was used at the end of the school day by the school gymnastic club. It was a special school. I had gotten used to the ease of its use and wanted the same in my new school. Unfortunately, although it was a new school it had already been built. If I had been involved in the planning for the new school, it could have been included. After a few years of talks with the school governors, who were keen, with the local council and their architects, it was eventually decided that the school did not have anywhere suitable for a sunken trampoline. I contacted the builders of the school who assured me that it could be done, but at a cost of £65,000. We did not have that kind of money. In 2010, I monitored and evaluated the use of therapies in our school. At the time the trampoline was being set up regularly in the hall and we had students with moderate learning difficulties who told me during my monitoring that they didn't understand why they couldn't use the trampoline in the hall. The fact that they were able to jump and do somersaults and enjoyed having their own trampolines at home made it seem unfair that only those who were being hoisted onto the trampoline were able to use it.

The rules used to be that where the bed is being used for trampolining, a ceiling height of 5 metres or 16 feet is required. If lower, the coach/therapist should always remain in contact with the student and not bounce higher than 30 centimetres or 1 foot. Where the bed is being used for therapeutic purposes, as in Rebound Therapy, the safe ceiling height must be determined by the coach/therapist within the risk assessment. The risk assessment should be shown to and agreed by the parents/carers before the therapy takes place. Please remember that risk assessments are done to protect everyone and can be used in a court of law.

As a result of the monitoring and evaluating exercise, I managed to raise 12,000 pounds to have a trampoline embedded in the school playground. Due to health and safety reasons, I could not allow those students to use the trampoline inside the school that had such short headspace, but I was darned if they would miss out on having the same opportunity of using a trampoline when in school. We later purchased mini trampolines too.

If your school does decide to go ahead with having a trampoline embedded in the floor inside the school, there are now several good contractors about who design and install them to the appropriate safety standard, but the local authority will need to be on board. If you want one embedded in the playground, then I highly recommend GL Jones Playgrounds of North Wales. They installed the trampoline in the photo as well as another playground equipment for us.

There should also be rules regarding what the school wishes students to wear whilst on the trampoline. Is it acceptable for students with PMLD to be taken to the trampoline and hoisted on in the clothes they are currently wearing, or should they have a routine where they are changed into a specific kit beforehand and are shoe-less? Or should that only apply to students who are ambulant? Buckles, zips, buttons, earrings and other accessories can damage the trampoline bed

Figure 9.1 Embedded outdoor playground trampoline

if they get caught in it. They can also injure the therapist, coach or student themselves if the student moves unexpectedly. Long hair should be tied back, and nails kept short as nails can get caught in the trampoline bed or in equipment being used.

There needs to be a school policy on suitable clothing for trampolining although you may well have a policy for PE that encompasses trampolining. If you don't treat the subject with respect, neither will the students.

What are the dress rules for the trampoline coach or therapist? In all the schools I have taught in, there are very strict rules. In my last school we bought all therapists T-shirts with a recognisable logo on it. Figure 9.2 shows the one for Rebound Therapy being worn. Therapists wear them with jogging bottoms and wear socks. You can purchase specific trampoline footwear from Winstrada and other recognised bodies.

If you currently work in a special school, you will be used to risk assessments. A photocopiable risk assessment appears at the end of this chapter. Please feel free to download and adapt to your school. They are there to protect staff and pupils and should be written up if you are ever concerned about using a piece of equipment or if you have concerns about a student attending a session, behaviour of a pupil, clothing being worn or the number of staff supervising. The risk assessment will inform you if the risks are too high and you can present the risk assessment to your

Figure 9.2 Trampoline therapist uniform

line manager if you have concerns that you feel haven't been addressed. Never be afraid to protect yourself and those in your care. A completed risk assessment that you may wish to adapt can be found at the end of this chapter.

The area around the trampoline should be clear. If you have a student on the trampoline whom you hoisted on from their wheelchair, then you will need to remove the wheelchair to a safe area of the room. If the room is small you may need to remove the chair outside until the session is over.

All schools have fire safety procedures and emergency evacuation procedures. These procedures should be shared regularly with staff and should be displayed somewhere prominent. A first aider should be available during any trampoline session. There should be an annual check of equipment by an independent specialist but also you should inspect for damage before allowing trampoline use for the day/session.

It is easy for me to accept that the staff I have worked with would not allow more than one student at a time on a trampoline. The room is also protected by a coded entry button so other students tempted by the trampoline cannot easily access the room. It makes sense for schools to have rules so here are some you can copy and paste onto a Rules Poster if you wish. This should be displayed prominently for all visitors, students and staff to see.

Figure 9.3 Rules for Schools

Resource 9.1 Trampoline Rules for Schools

The coach, teacher or therapist leading the session should ensure that:

1   Both student and coach/teacher/therapist are fit enough to take part in the session.
2   Surrounding matting is trip-free and equipment, including trampoline, is safe to use.

3   Eating or drinking on or around the trampoline is forbidden.
4   Socks or correct trampoline footwear should always be worn.
5   Long hair should be tied back securely.
6   Suitable clothing should be worn by staff and students.
7   No mobile phones allowed during sessions.
8   No smoking allowed.
9   No person with jewellery, false nails or body piercing is allowed on the trampoline.

10 Nails should be checked before a session commences (nothing worse than a ripped nail caught in trampoline webbing).

(Continued)

(Continued)

11 A proper programme with records must be available and completed for every student using the trampoline. These must be available to class teachers for use in school reports to parents.

12 Correct procedures for reporting accidents must be followed including immediate contact with parent/carer if a student is involved.

13 Accident forms must be completed after any accident and a copy given to the designated school lead in health and safety.

14 Risk assessments must be completed; a copy should be included in the trampoline file and a copy given to the school lead in health and safety.

15 Wait your turn.

16 No double bouncing is ever condoned. It is highly dangerous.

17 No one should fiddle with trampoline webbing and springs. If you see anyone doing so, report it immediately.

18 Correct mounting and dismounting once taught should always be followed. No one is allowed to bounce off a trampoline EVER.

19 Appropriate staffing levels must always be maintained.

20 Any observations to be agreed beforehand and observer to observe from designated position only.

21 Sand timers will be used to time some sessions to ensure sessions do not go over time allotted.

22 No equipment should be stored next to or under the bed at any time even for short periods of time.

Mini trampoline

Mini trampolines in schools do not pose the same risk as they are only 3 to 4 inches off the floor. Mini trampolines also have detachable bars so that if your students have coordination issues, you can keep the bar on for them to hold onto for balance.

A mini trampoline needs to be set up so that it is clear of any tables, chairs or other furniture so that if a student does fall off, they don't hit anything.

Clubs, parks and home trampolines

All clubs have their own policies and safety procedures and most of them follow recommended guidance and use readily available documents provided by the British Gymnastics organisation. These support clubs in obtaining DBS checks, having safe environments as well as rules and regulation templates. Please see the chapter on clubs for more information on clubs. The Rebound Therapy Association for Chartered Physiotherapists provides its own guidance for safe practice in Rebound Therapy (CSP 2016).

Trampoline parks have had bad press in recent years because they haven't been regulated and there have been reports of accidents. In 2017 ambulances were called out to 1,181 incidents across England – more than three per day because there are no safety regulations (BBC 2018). The International Association of Trampoline Parks (IATP) estimates 15 million people a year use its parks. The IATP worked with the British Standards Institute, the Royal Society for the Prevention of Accidents (RoSPA) and British Gymnastics to devise voluntary safety standards, and parks that become members of IATP must meet those standards now. It makes sense therefore for anyone thinking of attending a trampoline park to check out first whetherthe park belongs to the IATP. If it doesn't, then my advice would be – don't go there.

IATP also advises the following:

1   Never jump without a court monitor present.
2   Be certain to read and abide by all the rules and regulations posted throughout the park.
3   Make sure to watch the safety video provided or have a briefing from park staff.
4   Always be aware of your surroundings, and never jump around or near other jumpers.
5   If the park has a foam pit, make sure the foam is at or above the level of the trampoline.

Having a trampoline at home poses its own problems and safety hazards that are overall different to the problems encountered in schools. Please see chapter 8 on home trampolines for this important information.

All participants who have Down Syndrome and wish to participate in gymnastics activity (including trampoline) are required to be screened under the following guidelines:

> These guidelines have been prepared to assist coaches to understand the medical screening requirements for gymnasts with Down Syndrome. The aim of the screening is to provide access to gymnastics and trampolining for everyone who can benefit from involvement in this sport and who are at no greater risk than other gymnasts. All gymnasts with Down Syndrome **must** have approval from British Gymnastics before **any** participation in gymnastics or trampoline is permitted.

Participation in gymnastics and trampolining by people with Down Syndrome is permitted, subject to the following provisos:

- Parent/Guardian's consent is obtained (under 16's).
- There is no evidence of progressive myopathy in the person concerned.
- That neck flexion to allow the chin to rest on the chest is possible.
- That the person has good head/neck muscular control.

Screening must be undertaken by a qualified medical practitioner. Those who are eligible to undertake the necessary tests include General Practitioners, Orthopaedic or Paediatric Consultants, School Medical Officers/Doctors, Chartered Physiotherapists.

There should be no sign of progressive myopathy. Some signs of progressive myopathy are:

- Increase in muscle weakness
- Loss of sensation
- Onset of incontinence
- Alteration in muscle tone
- Decreasing co-ordination
- Diminishing kinaesthetic awareness
- Change in walking pattern
- Pins and needles

NB: Not all may be present, but any one of the above requires further investigation.

1   Neck flexion to allow the chin to rest on the chest: the person should be able to bend their head forwards sufficiently so that the chin rests on the chest.
2   That the person has good head/neck muscular control: This can be tested – the person lies on their back with legs straight and they are pulled to sitting position by their hands, with the examiner pulling from the front.

Table 9.1 Atlanto-Axial Screening Form

Approval for participation in gymnastics and trampoline gymnastics for person with Down Syndrome

Gymnast details:		
Name:		
Email address:		
Date of birth:	Male / Female	Ms / Mrs / Mr / Miss
Address:	Post code:	
BG Membership No: (if applicable)	Telephone:	
Club/School:	Region:	
Coach details:		
Name:		
BG Membership No:		

5 **Gymnast (16 & over) or parent/guardian consent: (under 16's) (Following medical clearance)**

I agree to my child/dependant participating in gymnastics and am fully aware of the risks involved in this sport.

NB: Please insert the parents/guardian's address below if different from that of the gymnast

Gymnast/Guardian signature:	
Where a gymnast is over 16 years of age and is unable to make an informed decision, a signature must be gained from the gymnast's guardian.	
Gymnast signature	Parent/Guardian address
Parent/Guardian (Print Name)	
Parent/Guardian (Signature)	

6 Screening

A qualified medical practitioner or chartered physiotherapist must complete the following tests and questions (delete as appropriate):	
1. Does the person show evidence of progressive Myopathy?	Yes / No
2. Does the person have poor head/neck muscular control?	Yes / No
3. Does the person's neck flexion allow the chin to rest on their chest?	Yes / No
Name:	
Designation:	
Address:	Practice stamp:
Signature:	

If a gymnast has a positive test (Yes) for any of the first two questions or a negative test (No) for question three, the individual will be excluded from participation in all gymnastics activity within British Gymnastics recognised environments.

7 **For BG Office Use:**

8 **Received by BG Office:**   Date:

Signature:

9 **Approved:**   Yes ☐   No ☐   (Tick appropriate)

10 Action required/notes:

11 **On completion of screening, one copy of the fully completed approval form must be forwarded to British Gymnastics.**

Please forward to:

AAI Medical Screening
British Gymnastics
Lilleshall National Sports Centre
Newport
Shropshire

TF10 9AT Further information regarding atlanto-axial subluxation can be gained from:

The Down's Syndrome Association   **Tel:** 0333 1212 300
Langdon Down Centre   **e-mail:** info@downs-syndrome.org.uk
2a Langdon Park   **Web:** www.downs-syndrome.org.uk
Teddington
TW11 9PS   Reg. Charity No: 1061474

Source: Atlanto-Axial screening information sheet adapted from www.british-gymnastics.org/ . . . /9316-atlanto-axial-information-pack-1/file PDF file

Table 9.2 Trampoline Risk Assessment Resource

Directorate	Education	Activity (Brief Description)		Trampoline therapy	
Service	Education	People at Risk		Pupils and staff	
Location	Special school	Date		Review Date	
Assessor		Issue Number		1	
Item No	Hazard (Include Defects)	RISK RATING (without controls) High/ Medium/ Low	Existing Control Measures		RISK RATING (with existing controls) High/ Medium/ Low
1	Setting up and taking down of trampolines (Serious Injury – Broken bones/Muscle Strains)	High	Trampoline set up permanently in designated room. Room well organised.		Low
2	Falling off trampoline (Serious Injury – Death/Broken bones/ Muscle Strains)	High	Current students have limited movement due to their needs and those able to stand are assisted to jump in the middle of the bed. This allows for the required amount of safe distance on the trampoline. There will also be spotters placed at the side of the trampoline.		Low
3	Improper dismount (Serious Injury – Broken bones/Muscle Strains)	High	Students are always to be assisted to climb on and off the trampoline.		Low
4	More than one person jumping at a time (Falling or collisions resulting in Serious Injury – Broken bones/Muscle Strains)	High	Only one participant to be on the trampoline at any given time other than a suitably qualified coach/therapist.		Low

(Continued)

5	Injury/pregnancy (Aggravating existing injury resulting in Serious Injury – Death/Broken bones/ Muscle Strains; Miscarriage in pregnant women)	High	Staff and/or students suffering from back or neck pain are advised not to participate as this may aggravate or worsen the injury. Pregnant women are not to participate at all in trampoline. People suffering from broken bones or recovering from surgery will require a doctor's letter stating their injury has fully healed and are able to use the trampoline.	Low
6	Disabilities	Medium	All students require a consent form signed by parents (and in some cases also their doctor) before they may go on a trampoline.	Low
7	Not being able to follow instructions (Incorrect practice resulting in Serious Injury – Broken bones/Muscle Strains)	High	Teacher ready to explain again when something not understood and communicates in line with students' level of understanding. Students not adhering to the rules will be asked to dismount the trampoline safely and will not be permitted to continue.	Low
8	Observers distracting students/staff (Loss of concentration resulting in Serious Injury – Death/Broken bones/Muscle Strains)	High	Under no circumstance are observers allowed to interfere with students unless it is to keep them safe by spotting them back onto trampoline. Observations can only happen if pre-booked and observers must remain silent whilst the session is in progress.	Low
9	Damaged or faulty equipment, including overhead hoist (Serious Injury – Death/Broken bones/ Muscle Strains)	High	Ensure school checks are carried out and recorded. Governors should be given view of last safety check or maintenance report at each term's governor committee meeting.	Low
10	Placement of trampoline (falling/ obstructions in event of emergency evacuation resulting in serious injury – Death/Broken bones/Muscle Strains)	High	Trampolines must be set up away from the fire exits. Must be set up with enough space to allow for natural movement of beds during use. Height restrictions for jumping must be adhered to.	Low

#	Hazard	Risk	Control Measures	Residual
11	Supervision of Injury and First Aid Control (Cross Infection or making an injury worse)	High	Ensure correct school first aid procedures are followed. Senior management staff to be made aware of any incident or injury during trampoline sessions.	Low
12	Child Protection (Coach/therapist or Staff Accused/Children Harmed)	High	Schools to ensure any staff working at the school are appropriately trained and hold current DBS checks. Relevant notices will be displayed in room.	Low
13	Clothing/Footwear and Jewellery (Falling or snagging resulting in Serious Injury – Broken bones/Muscle Strains)	High	Students should wear correct attire and footwear (trampoline shoes or non-slip socks). Student's parents and teacher will be given information on what the student needs to wear and reminded that the student cannot take part if they do not have this (due to health and safety). *All jewellery must be removed, and hair tied back securely.*	Low
14	Spotting (Serious Injury – Death/Head injury/Broken bones/Muscle Strains)	High	Trained spotters will be situated on all sides which are not protected by alternative safety measures. Trampoline lead must ensure spotters are paying full attention.	Low
15	Underneath trampolines (Serious Injury – Death/Head injury/Broken bones/Muscle Strains)	High	Students should not go underneath trampolines at any time and should be prevented from swinging on the frame edge under the side of trampoline.	Low

10 | Trampolining clubs, parks and after school provision

In this chapter we look at trampoline parks and clubs that support those with learning differences. These parks and clubs are sometimes used by schools to deliver sessions that the schools themselves do not have the facilities to deliver. They are also used by the clubs themselves that compete and by families of those with differing learning and physical disabilities who may use the park or club on an ad hoc basis. There are many more of these parks and clubs available and the ones I refer to are just some of those I contacted or visited. Some are excellent and some need a posse of parents reminding them of the rights of the child. I have given links to the websites, but it is worth bearing in mind that websites are not always regularly updated, and my advice would always be to contact them by phone or email before visiting.

At the end of this chapter I tell you how I managed to set up an after school club for young persons and adults with learning disabilities in the local community at our school. The club provides trampoline sessions for those that attend, and it is a very popular leisure pursuit. At the end of this chapter I give you the business plan I wrote, and other documents devised so that you may copy them if you wish to set up your own club. The BG website and the home nations disability sports organisations also provide you with the resources to set up your own club. For your club to become a member of the British Gymnastics organisation (BG), there are a few key roles that you must have in place beforehand. Information on these roles can be found on its website. It offers bespoke coach education and experienced British Gymnastic staff who can offer technical knowledge and guidance on the set-up and sustainability of a trampoline club. It provides a range of resources for the promotion and marketing of sessions and the templates and logos to communicate the partnership with British Gymnastics. All guidance and support for anyone considering setting up a club can be found on its website. I have set up different clubs for disabled in the past without any support and I am amazed at how much easier the BG organisation makes it and the protection that it gives you.

Disability Sport Wales website provides INSPORT clubs standards. The basic standard is called Ribbon. This is followed by Bronze, Silver and Gold. INSPORT provides documents which explain the requirements for each level, and they are useful documents for anyone wishing to set up a trampoline club to ensure that you are inclusive. As you develop as a club, you move up the levels to eventually become a Gold Standard Club. The DSW promotes INSPORT clubs on its website. This means that anyone looking for a club that caters for those with disabilities will know which clubs in Wales cater for their needs.

Links to its website and other home nations disability sports organisations and resources can be found in chapter 11.

It is far easier to be able to take your child or adult with learning differences to an accessible established club or park but sometimes you may feel that it may not meet their needs. You may be a governor, school manager, social worker, health worker or local authority official who wishes to use your local special school that already has a trampoline, hoists, necessary resources and willing trained staff to enable you to set up your own club. I urge you to bite the bullet and make use of a building and its facilities that often remains empty once the school day ends.

There are some fantastic trampoline clubs and parks around that cater for people with additional learning needs. I visited many and spoke to several officials at these parks and clubs. The officials I spoke to were passionate about giving everybody the opportunity to enjoy the health benefits of trampolining. Every single time I came away from those meetings humbled by their dedication to making the world a better place where those with disabilities can have access to the same leisure pursuits we ordinary folk take for granted.

Trampoline parks

The first trampoline clubs and parks were established in America in 1959. They took America by storm. Initially they were hugely popular in America and big money spinners, but they weren't regulated at all. Accidents and even deaths occurred and in the 1970s trampoline clubs in America fell out of favour.

History can repeat itself but as the writer and philosopher George Santayana would say:

'Those who cannot remember the past are condemned to repeat it'.

(Internet Encyclopedia of Philosophy)

Today trampoline parks are popular across the world but the International Association of Trampoline Parks (IATP) is striving to ensure better regulation so that history does not repeat itself. It also claims that the health benefits (cardiovascular, muscular, coordination, social interaction) of active bouncing far outweigh the negatives (IATP 2019).

Jump in Trampoline Parks are registered with IATP and offer relaxed sessions using the trampoline for those with additional needs. The session I watched seem perfect for people of all ages with disabilities and their families to enjoy. At present they don't have hoists but have ramps leading onto the trampolines. All their parks have disabled access and disabled toilets. Most only have baby changing facilities and not disabled changing facilities, which is a shame, though I was reassured that it would be something on their list of priorities. They provide sessions which include soft lighting and soothing music for a relaxed, safe and sensory experience. Jump In management ask you to work with them so that they can create the perfect therapeutic trampoline session for your children and adults with additional needs. I spoke with a regular member of staff about the changing room situation and she felt confident that she could speak with head office to prioritise it immediately. A company that gives its staff confidence to be able to do that is a company worth working for.

One of their trampoline parks based in Leamington has launched Rebound Therapy classes aimed at children and adults with autism or heightened sensory needs. Rebound Therapy–qualified instructors are on hand to work either one to one or in groups after a full assessment of needs is carried out. These parks are situated throughout England and Scotland and carers accompanying anyone with a disability can jump for free. Its website is www.gojumpin.com/

In the *Cornfield* magazine July 2019 edition (p. 18) Rob Borg, a Jump In regional manager, said:

> Trampolines at our parks offer great physio benefits for those with low muscle tone who need to maintain/build their core strength. This is because trampolines encourage the participant to constantly correct their balance when jumping and landing. This also helps with co-ordination which has been linked to learning and neurological development. Special needs schools and day centres have reported on how the trampoline has great benefits for autistic children and adults with heightened sensory needs.

Officials at Gravity Trampoline parks told me that their staff had been trained to appreciate that trampolining has been shown to help with a wide range of sensory, developmental and physical disabilities. In its disability sessions, the whole park and its facilities are made exclusively available to members of recognised disabled groups and societies that cater for a wide range of disabilities and there are set times that the park is made available. There is disabled access and lifts. They provide specialist equipment such as sensory tents and balls. Their tailored sessions have specially trained marshals and offer a completely dedicated yet fun environment focussed on sensory engagement, offering therapeutic exercise to participants. They work closely with organisations such as the National Autistic Society. At present they have no hoist or ramp facilities and no specific changing facilities for those who are physically disabled. The website is www.gravity-uk.com/

There are many other trampoline parks that cater for those with additional needs. Jump360 for instance, offers Jump Support sessions dedicated for individuals with additional needs or disabilities. Those with additional needs can attend any of the general sessions (if they are 5 or older). If they attend a general session they are provided with a golden V.I.P wristband in addition to the coloured wristband for their session, alerting court marshals that this individual may require extra care or attention. The carer(s) are given a golden V.I.P wrist band to signify that although they are not taking part in the Jump session, they have been cleared to enter the arena and supervise/assist when needed. You will need to contact individual parks to check if they have hoists and disabled changing facilities. Lifts are not available in all locations. The website is www.jump360.co.uk/

Flip Out Trampoline Parks have disabled toilets but only baby changing facilities and require a doctor's note that specifies your child can go on a trampoline. The website is www.flipout.co.uk

Jump Space Trampoline Park caters specifically for disabled and their families. It has hoists, lifts, disabled toilets and changing facilities. It has a sensory room and a soft play area. There are trampoline classes and Rebound Therapy sessions. It is based in Stockport. The website is www.jumpspace.org.uk

Jump Evolution based in Romford, Essex, have quiet sensory areas, disabled changing facilities, wheelchair ramps, PEC 'stop and go' signs, and you can be fast-tracked into the park. The website is www.jumpevolution.co.uk

The general rule for any trampoline park states that there should only be one person on a trampoline bed at any one given time. Management in most parks understand some guests will require one-on-one assistance with their carer on the trampoline. If in doubt contact the park beforehand. There are so many parks in the UK now that you are sure to find one that will meet your requirements.

Clubs

There are trampoline clubs around the UK that cater for people with all kinds of impairments and health conditions. Many clubs offer free taster sessions that you can take your child or young adult to. I managed to visit some clubs in the UK and to talk to some club officials. I wanted to see what they provided for those with profound and multiple disabilities and if they had the facilities to cater for them. I wanted to see if they encouraged those with learning differences such as autism and attention deficit hyperactive disorder to compete and at what level. I already know from my own experiences over the years that trampolining is an activity that people of all ages and disabilities enjoy. The website www.theautismdirectory.com gives links to trampoline clubs and parks that its members have used.

The British Gymnastics (BG) organisation website (www.british-gymnastics.org) provides lists and links to approved clubs run at leisure centres and schools. There are others too but the good thing about attending one approved of by the organisation is that you can be confident that they have all the necessary policies and procedures in place that protects the children from your school or your child or adult.

There are some amazing clubs that deliver both therapeutic trampolining, often in the form of Rebound Therapy (if a suitably trained person is available), and basic trampolining leading on to competitive trampolining for children with disabilities. Many of the clubs advertise that they run sessions for able bodies and disabled. You will need to contact the club before attending as some of the clubs advertised on the BG website no longer operate. When I contacted some of the club officials of those that no longer operate, I was told that it was from lack of available coaches trained to meet the needs of children with disabilities.

Following are my top five clubs, in no order, and if you are lucky enough to live near to one of them, then pop along – you will not be disappointed.

- The Northamptonshire Trampoline Gymnastics Academy (NTGA) in 2019 has 23 hours per week of trampoline classes/sessions for groups, organisations, schools and individuals with special needs and it is called the Ability Zone Programme. The programme has around 80 members with special needs and has been running formally for over 12 years, growing each year, with some of their partnerships that go back almost 20 years.

The academy is a premier UK club and a British Gymnastics High Performance Centre, with a world-class coaching team that produces success at Regional, National, European, World and Olympic level. Ross Whittaker, the 2019 director of the club, told me that currently, none of the Ability Zone members compete; however it's something they have considered and review periodically. They have previously attended a few friendly competitions; however, they found the Disability Competition Structure was more geared towards physical disability and the format/rules/expectations did not suit most members. NTGA is passionate about the rights of all its members and the staff also told me they believe that British Gymnastics is adding more categories to become more inclusive and the NTGA will follow that up when it happens for its members that are interested. The website is www.ntga.co.uk

- In recent years, Preston City Trampoline Club worked with UK Deaf Sport to complete its new DEAFinitely Inclusive accreditation scheme. Through the scheme, the club identified and addressed many of the barriers that deaf people can face when wanting to take part in gymnastics. To ensure the club sessions are inclusive for anyone who uses sign language, club coaches have attended communication courses in order to support them. They deliver Rebound Therapy sessions following the Winstrada programme but find that often a trampoline programme doesn't record the kind of progress that the coaches notice. For instance, one of the students recently managed to walk up the steps to the trampoline and stand on the trampoline for the first time. Everyone at the centre went home smiling that day. The student was so excited by his own achievement that he was still 'wired' when he left. That was an achievement that couldn't be recorded but will stay in people's memories.

At the present time the club has a member with autism who is competing in the National competitions. Members also compete in the trampoline league. The club holds demonstration days on a couple of weekends each year when relatives and friends are invited along to see what members can achieve. These weekends are very popular.

Colin Robson, the 2019 director, told me that the one difficulty they find with their members who have a learning disability is their ability to transition and this can affect their involvement in competitions. There are sometimes the usual barriers to competing such as financial and family concerns about being away from home that all people face but having a disability increases the magnitude of those concerns. They may be able to perform brilliantly at Preston City Trampoline Club but put them in a different club, with a different set-up, with different faces and with the pressures of a competition, and you could be not just heading for failure but perhaps even a meltdown.

The club is twinned with another trampoline club in Germany and the members who take part in these exchanges have been supported and prepared well in advance so that they have had positive experiences.

The club uses both the Winstrada Rebound Therapy system and the British Gymnastics system and these may act as prompts as often the club will adapt what is available to meet the needs of individuals. The club strives to meet each member's potential and the process is very organic. If a coach feels that something can be tried, then just because the person is labelled disabled doesn't mean the person would be prevented from doing it.

The club provides a drop-in session on Saturdays for children with autism aged 3–11 and their siblings. It has a sensory room that can also be used and a separate but large trampolining room for those who need a quieter room. This room also has sensory lighting and sensory equipment. The club is open every weekday for use by disabled groups or individuals and I saw it in action mid-week. Schools who cannot afford to deliver trampolining in their own building will, for a reasonable fee, use the club and its coaches during school hours.

The club has a café area that parents and carers use whilst the member is having a trampoline session with a coach. The café area is in sight of the trampolines in the main trampoline hall so that if a member needs support the carer or parent may be called. Parents appreciate having time to socialise with other parents. There are disabled toilets, disabled changing beds, and the club is spotlessly clean. The care shown towards an autistic adult by everyone at the club whilst I was there demonstrated the whole ethos of the club. It is second to none. The website is www.pctc.org.uk/disabilities/

- Twisters is a trampoline club based in Cardiff. Twisters is a Gold Standard INSPORT club (please see chapter 10 for more information on INSPORT) and it was voted club of the year for 2019. It is a fantastic well-respected trampoline club that you would want to send your trampoline enthusiast to if you lived near Cardiff. It is also the place to send someone who has PMLD. On the day I visited I was able to observe clients with PMLD enjoying the use of the trampoline with their carers. It was a joy to watch.

Heather Sargent set up rebounders for those with disabilities in 2002. She originally set it up for those who were unable or didn't feel comfortable joining mainstream classes. The first inclusive class was held for six children with coordination difficulties but within six weeks a second class was needed, and demand grew, and more classes set up. In 2008 Rebounders was set up as a charity and opened its own doors in Ocean Park, Cardiff. In 2013 an associated club called Twisters was formed by Heather at the site.

It offers trampolining sessions for everyone, including both recreational classes and regional and national development plan (NDP) competitive classes. It caters for all ages from pre-school to adult, and all abilities from PMLD to elite competitors. Other clubs send the members they find do not fit into their clubs to Heather.

All sessions are coached by fully qualified British Gymnastics Coaches. Members are grouped according to their ability in disability-specific or inclusive recreational and competitive classes. They enter both Regional and National competitions and can boast both Welsh and British Schools Champions and Welsh National Champions over the past couple of years. They claimed third place in the team event at the British Veterans Adult Competition in 2016 and 2017. Heather's club currently has 230 that attend with a disability; 40 of these take part in competitions. There is a disability squad comprising the most able trampolinists. Two members with ADHD are competing at a national level and are aiming to be selected for the GB squad. Heather is keen to get trampolining into the Special Olympics. Heather devised the club's own competition called Tramp-Ability based on the BG awards but broken down into achievable goals. Some of the members attend specifically to enter the competitions. Heather invites other clubs to compete in the Tramp-Ability competitions. It would be great if Heather could advertise her programme in the same way that Winstrada and Rebound Therapy.org advertise their progression resources (see chapter 10 for more information on these).

As well as people being able to go along to Twisters based in Cardiff, Heather sends coaches out to schools to run classes during and after the school day. The website is www.twisterssw.club

- I took a group of school children to stay at the Wingate Centre to use its trampolining facilities in Wrenbury Cheshire almost 20 years ago and it is still going strong. The centre has an extensive range of indoor and outdoor recreational facilities including a 7.000-square-foot gymnasium, three trampolines, a sensory room, an extensive range of soft play equipment, three acres of gardens complete with a Trim Trail, Play Dale Adventure playground, an all-weather playground and sensory garden. At least one of the trampolines is embedded in the floor. It has excellent changing facilities for those with disabilities. Rebound Therapy classes are delivered and schools or individuals can book sessions throughout the week. The Olympic trampoline Silver Medallist Bryony Page is a vice president of the charity, and she used to train there as a child. Bryony says, 'It's a special and unique place that allows children with and without disabilities to keep active, learn new key life and social skills, and most of all have fun!' The website is www.thewingatecentre.co.uk

- OXSRAD is a Disability Sports and Leisure Centre in Oxford and a registered charity. It was first established by Alan Porter-Smith MBE in 1988 and officially opened by the Princess of Wales in 1989. OXSRAD is an inclusive centre that integrates people with disabilities through sport and recreation. It has some great facilities including a gym with specialised equipment, a sensory room, therapy room, café and a sports hall that is home to its Rebound Therapy sessions. It has disabled changing facilities and there is step-free access throughout the building. Staff receive disability awareness training. Prince Harry attended a Rebound Therapy session there in 2019. The prince observed the trampoline session at the side of the trampoline and chatted afterwards to both staff and members. The website is www.oxsrad.org

Some other clubs that I didn't get to visit but have been recommended to me for families of children with additional learning needs are listed next.

Flying High Trampolining Club (FHTC), based at Denbigh Leisure Centre in North Wales, is a volunteer-run club. The club provides opportunities for children and adults diagnosed with visual impairment, physical disability such as cerebral palsy and learning difficulties including ASD and ADHD to enjoy the mental and physical health benefits of trampolining while making new friends. The club is available for contact through disabilitysportwales.com or can be contacted at flyinghigh@outlook.com.

Whizz-Kids is a national charity that supports disabled children. It has a growing network of clubs that offer fun activities for all children with disabilities. Activities depend on where the clubs are run and what resources are available, but they often include bouncy castles and trampolining.

Orchard Trust offers a trampoline therapy called 'stealth physio'. The Orchard is an independent charity established in 1989 to support the involvement, independence and development of people with disabilities. The Trust has a few care homes and supported living homes in the Forest of Dean, supporting people across Gloucestershire, Monmouthshire and Herefordshire areas.

Some local ordinary leisure centres that have trampolines do run trampoline sessions in specific time slots for people diagnosed with autism or ADHD for example, but these tend to be for one hour per week, usually on a Saturday, and the advice, as always, is to ring first.

If you put in your postcode on its website (www.british-gymnastics.org/discover/trampoline), British Gymnastics will send you to the nearest disability trampoline club in your region. You will need to phone first before visiting as sometimes the opening times are limited or they no longer operate. I would hate you to have a wasted journey particularly if you have been looking forward to it.

As head of a special school (from 2009 to 2019) with fantastic resources, I was committed to providing After School Provision (ASP) for adults with learning disabilities. Reinders argues for a paradigm shift in our relation to people with profound and multiple learning difficulties (PMLD) (Reinders 2008). Whilst I agree wholeheartedly with him, I also believe there needs to be a paradigm shift in how we view and use special schools. Special schools should not be abolished (Henderson 1999) but their trampoline rooms and other therapy rooms should be available to adults with disabilities after school hours.

Adults with severe learning difficulties (SLD) or PMLD are amongst the most disadvantaged in society. The prejudice, discrimination and low expectations faced by people with SLD or PMLD and their families must be addressed for real inclusion in society and for them to have real access to lifelong learning. I have seen the difference trampolining has made to students' ability to learn. Inclusion should be about including the use of schools with specialist resources for any person in society who would benefit from those resources. Inclusion should be about joined up working between social services, health and education so that the facilities in a special school are available 24/7 to those who need them.

All people, no matter what their disability, have a right to communicate and participate in the life of their local community as enshrined in the UN Convention on Human Rights. However, knowing their rights is of no use to the disabled person or their parents if either are unable to make it happen. The Children and Families Act 2014 allows us to dream of effective partnership working at all levels guaranteeing the person-centred approach it aspires to deliver from the large public investment in learning disability services. In our dreams we see a bright future. In these exponential times, where the world is changing rapidly as we speak, how can we ensure that the nightmare of isolation and marginalisation no longer exists for the forgotten people of our society?

Schools today that cater specifically for children with SLD or PMLD often have state-of-the-art facilities that adults with the same disabilities as these children never got the chance to experience.

Baroness Warnock stated in 2010 (Warnock et al. 2010) that it was never her intention for special schools to be abolished. However, successive governments since 1978 have argued against their existence in a modern inclusive society,

> But there is, in this modern world, a growing need for buildings, call them what you will, that provide specialist facilities such as hydrotherapy pools, trampoline rooms, music therapy rooms, physiotherapy rooms, reflexology rooms, dark rooms, Virtual Reality rooms, Vibro acoustic beds, eye gaze facilities and more. All with overhead hoists, because it is a fact that data and assumptions from the Centre for Disability Research (CeDR) in 2009 suggested sustained and accelerating growth in the numbers of adults with PMLD in England over the time period 2009–2026 with an average annual percentage increase of 1.8%.
>
> (Emerson 2009)

Inclusion means not hidden away from society. Special schools should not be abolished but should stand loud and proud in society at large and be recognised as having something valuable to offer. A place where people make the effort to go to make and meet friends and enjoy taking part on educational and leisure pursuits where the facilities meet the needs of the users. Disabled children are rarely chosen as friends by able-bodied children, and adults with PMLD live largely friendless lives (Reinders 2008).

We should not be concerned about ensuring we include children and adults with PMLD in activities that we enjoy and that they will possibly gain nothing from (although the well-meaning person may well feel better for having attempted to include them), but we should concern ourselves in making the effort to be included in an activity the person with PMLD appears to enjoy for themselves. The ordinary person should not be concerned with showing beneficence towards those with SLD or PMLD but perhaps instead should be concerned with a fundamental re-evaluation of life itself so that we work towards becoming a community of equals where friendships just happen.

It is well known that before any of us can learn and develop we need to be in the right frame of mind to do so. Governments throughout the world promote wellbeing in schools to ensure pupils realise their potential, and schools in the UK are inspected on how they manage pupil's wellbeing. What about the wellbeing of adults with autism ASD, SLD or PMLD?

There are physical, psychological and social benefits of leisure that contribute to health and wellbeing. Adults with ASD, SLD and PMLD have the same needs and therefore gain from the same education and leisure facilities that children who now attend new special schools benefit from. These facilities can help improve the health and wellbeing, physical, mental and emotional, for people with complex needs and their families, through active participation.

One of the many health inequalities facing adults with ASD, SLD and PMLD is reduced access to regular exercise and therapies. The effect of a therapy that is appropriate will reduce spinal problems, improve neuropsychological functioning whilst increasing bone mass and muscle strength. This can, in turn, improve lung capacity and in general reduce likelihood of infection, giving a holistic sense of wellness.

I firmly believe that special schools should be used by the local authority as they already use some secondary school's leisure facilities for after school hours. I believe the new modern special schools can provide meaningful, accessible leisure sessions to people with the most profound needs, who are often excluded from the more mainstream leisure initiatives which people with less severe disabilities can access.

It is my vision that modern special schools will belong to the local community becoming a part of a diversity of provision to meet a continuum of need through the sharing of effective practice, the development of a culture of inclusion within shared local communities and the promotion of inclusive leisure, learning and wellbeing.

I worked closely with adult services for a few years and developed the provision so that in 2014 we were delivering different therapies to adults on three evenings a week. We had a waiting list of adults with learning difficulties who wished to attend. In August 2014 I wrote and submitted a business plan to the Morgan Foundation, a charity that supports those with disabilities, with the hope that the school could have a grant to extend the provision to five nights a week, 4pm to 7pm, and on a Saturday. The bid was successful. However, Friends of Ysgol Pen Coch (our PTA) did not have enough members to oversee the grant.

I co-incidentally met up with a representative from the well-known Crossroads charity and the bid was resubmitted to include its involvement. Again, the bid was successful. A copy of the successful business plan is shown on the following pages so that anyone may copy it.

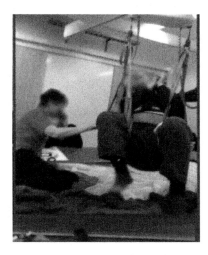

Figure 10.1 Using an overhead hoist with the trampoline

A list of useful forms, policies and documents that were devised are also shown and may be copied. I have removed all photos and named references so that you may add your own. The grant was for three years and the hope is that the ASP will sustain itself. I was very grateful to Crossroads and hope that this partnership becomes a template that can be rolled out by the charity across other special schools in Wales. Trampolining was a very popular activity for the adults with learning disabilities and it is delivered every evening that the after school club is open.

Photocopiable resources and tables

1   Business Plan to gain funding for After School Therapies Club
2   Referral and Assessment Form
3   Emergency Contact Information
4   Hiring of School Premises Policy and Fee Structure
5   Service Level Agreement

Resource 10.1 Business Plan to gain funding for After School Therapies Club

After School Provision Club

Business Plan 2015–16

Ange Anderson

Well-being for Life

Introduction

This Business Plan has been developed in consultation with the working party and sets out *our adult support* vision, aims and values together with our key objectives for 2015/16.

This business plan supports the leisure activities to enhance the quality of lives and improve the health of those adults with severe or profound learning difficulties living in the local community that we serve.

The business plan also adopts the ethos of efficient working through innovation and partnership working.

local priorities regarding the Social Services & Well-being (Wales) Act 2015. Our Business Plan supports the outcomes of our Community Planning Partners as well as other relevant national initiatives.

An outline

The building opened in September 2009 and is a North Wales special school. It is a non-profit organisation with charitable status, with after school facilities set up to benefit the community.

The school is responsible for the strategic and operational management of educational and leisure facilities within the building. The headteacher works in partnership with the Social Services Support Manager for Learning Disabilities, and the NHS Community Nurse for learning disabled adults to provide leisure, educational and well-being facilities for learning disabled adults in the local community.

These facilities provide a strong infrastructure of community leisure for adults with learning difficulties.

WHAT DO WE OFFER?
Hydrotherapy
Trampoline Therapy
Therapeutic Music
Vibro-acoustic Therapy
Reflexology

WHAT DO WE OFFER?
Hoisting facilities
Changing facilities
Staff experienced in working with those with ALN
Qualified therapists
Resources
Staff room

In delivering its services the school works with many partners including the local County Council, NHS, and Social Services. In doing so we feel that we contribute to the local Community Plan, and to the outcomes and priorities set out in the Welsh Government's Act for Social Services and Well-being.

The day-to-day operations of the school are managed by the Senior Management Team (Executive) led by the Headteacher who is given strategic direction by the governing body. The governing body have a duty to act in the interests of the school and operate in accordance with its objects and purposes.

The school employs 6 staff for its services to adults with learning difficulties. Due to the demand for the use of these facilities by learning disabled adults, the partnership is concerned that it will not be able to continue without a manager employed to manage the use of the facilities.

Review of 2014/15

2014/15 was a challenging year for us, but a rewarding one too. The main challenges we faced were:

- Funding: Due to severe pressure on budget it is impossible for school, NHS or Social Services to fund the management of the learning disabled adult service which has grown during the year.
- Costs: Many costs are incurred as therapy staff require payment which cannot be taken from the budget allocated to the school. The school receives no designated budget for its pool costs or its energy costs, which are substantial. Currently the costs are being met by the charges made for the use of the facilities.
- Closure of facilities: Due to no designated manager of the service, the facilities are not available to adults with learning disabilities during weekends and school holiday periods. This causes upset to clients who do not understand why they cannot access the facilities on which they have come to depend.

On a positive note, notable highlights of the year were:

- Growth in Usage: There are currently no year-on-year comparisons as we have only been operating for a year. What we do know, however, is that the total number of adults

(Continued)

(Continued)

attending therapies since September 2014 has increased by 300% in 2015 and income has grown accordingly (and as there were no price increases this represents growth in custom).

- Operating Surplus: We are projecting that we will conclude the financial year with a modest operating surplus. Surpluses are reinvested back into the facilities and services for the adults with learning disability in the community benefit.
- Visit by Wales Assembly Member Aled Roberts pledged his support: https://twitter.com/AledRobertsAM/status/617296470279110657
- Taster Therapy Evenings: In partnership with the local authority's support manager for adults with learning disabilities, and the local authority's community learning disability nurse, we introduced different therapies that learning disabled adults could choose to try out and decide if they wanted to attend weekly/regularly. The therapy taster evening proved very popular and now 40-plus learning disabled adults attend outside of school time.

Key to the continued growth in usage is investment in facilities and services for our learning disabled pupils and disabled community attending local schools (the by-product of this is that the learning disabled adults in the local community are able to benefit too when we consider that the pupils attending our school will possibly become the learning disabled adults of the future). The school has invested in:

- A Vibro-acoustic Therapy room was introduced which contains a water-bed connected to an audio centre with specialist Somatron music.
- The cookery room was converted into a community room which parents of pupils use, and carers for learning disabled adults now use while their clients are receiving therapeutic input.
- A new trampoline room is currently being constructed from the former school library to include an overhead hoist and a trampoline in the floor so that height restrictions are reduced.

The partnership intends to:

Assess the Social Return on Investment (SROI): For the first time we intend to carry out an assessment of the impact we are making in the local authority's learning disabled community. We believe that the study will reveal that (in financial year 2015/16) for every £1 we spend there is £2 of economic and social benefit in our communities.

Assess the health and well-being impact on adults with learning disabilities in the community: We intend to carry out an assessment of the impact we are making on the health and well-being of the local learning disabled community. We believe that the study will reveal that the health and well-being of all adults with learning disabilities using the school facilities has improved.

The partnership needs:

> Charitable funding to employ a manager to run the facilities after school and at weekends for learning disabled adult use.

Analysis of need

Current leisure and well-being provision in the local authority for adults with learning disabilities (excluding facilities at the school).

The estimated number of adults with learning disabilities in this local authority in 2015 is 350. Of those 54 have PMLD, 22 have sensory needs and 28 are described as having behaviours which challenge.

Daytime

Individuals may attend traditional day (work) service which is managed by the local authority. These are at the local day centre, Castle connections, Estuary Crafts, Creftai Cariad, Tri fforyd, Abbey Metal, Freshfields and Rowleys Pantry. Some are supported in work placements whilst others use direct payments to secure their own services or leisure requirements as well as out-of-county placement or the Clocktower.

Evening

Leisure activities include discos provided by Ranch/Zoom, Buzz Club and Contact Club; Drama group provided by Buzzah; Mencap swimming sessions at Connahs Quay pool once a week; Deeside college sports; 10-pin bowling co-ordinated by Learning Disabilities group; Emerge Arts.

Data and assumptions from the Centre for Disability Research (CeDR) in 2009 suggested sustained and accelerated growth in the numbers of adults with PMLD in England over the time period 2009–2026 with an average annual percent increase of 1.8% (Emerson 2009). There is no data currently available for Wales. It is worth noting that the above provision does not cater for the actual needs of adults with PMLD.

Partnership working – 'making the connections'

We recognise that we can have far greater impact when we work closely with partners who share a common purpose, and with limited resources we can achieve more when there

(Continued)

(Continued)

is joined-up thinking and joined-up delivery. To achieve this, our school will develop a strategic alliance with key partners, continue to work with other partners and develop and strengthen operational relationships that add value.

We will develop a **Strategic Alliance** with:

Learning Disability Group
BCUHB
The local authority forum for learning disabilities

This business plan and resulting action plans will align with those of our strategic partners. We will demonstrate our achievements by regular performance reporting.

We will also be active participants in strategic groups, and we will continue to work in partnership with organisations to deliver shared objectives. Such organisations include:

The local authority learning disabled adult services
Mencap; the school governing body
Cartrefni; the school's parent association

Vision, aims and values

Our vision

Our Mission is *'to offer an excellent sport, therapeutic and leisure service that is fun and improves the lives of people 0with Profound and severe learning disabilities in the community we serve'*.

Our Vision is that by 2016 we will be:

> An organisation that is fully engaged with its customers, community and partners, and responsive to their needs.

Our aims

We have 10 Strategic Aims:

1   To **contribute to the shared outcomes of our partners**
2   To provide **opportunities and access** for adults with learning disabilities in our community to reach their desired level of **achievement and well-being**

3   To provide a **safe and enjoyable experience** for all

4   To deliver **an excellent service**, and to search out and adopt **best practice** methods

5   To become **a role model in positive partnering** between health, education and social services

6   To build and maintain **a successful business** that meets financial expectations

7   To **maximise opportunities** that arise or are created **to develop and grow** the business

8   To create a brand that stands for **quality and consistency**

9   To be recognised by our employees as **an excellent organisation to work for**

10   To adopt the principles of **best value and continuous improvement** in all that we do

Our values

Our school has high standards, and we will adopt the following values and principles in dealings with clients, colleagues and partners:

- We will act with integrity and show respect.
- We will be honest and open.
- We will listen, and put people at the heart of the decisions we make.
- We will be accountable for our actions.
- We will endeavour to be fair and equal, and be sensitive to the differences between people.

12 key objectives

These are our key objectives for the next year.

Contribute to the shared outcomes of our partners

1   To demonstrate our impact to partners

2   To be a more outward looking organisation

Opportunities and access for all

3   To engage with the learning disabled community to better understand their needs

4   To develop programming at facilities so that it meets the needs of the community

5   To increase levels of participation

A safe and enjoyable experience

6   To ensure the School Health and Safety Policy continues to be properly implemented

(Continued)

(*Continued*)

An excellent service that adopts best practice

7   To reduce energy consumption
8   To encourage sustainable practices

A successful business

9   To be a financially sustainable organisation

Maximise opportunities to develop and grow

10   To research opportunities to develop and grow the business

Quality and consistency

11   To have in place a quality model that drives improvement

Appendix – Budget for 2014–15[1]

Table 10a.1 Budget Apr 2014–Apr 2015

Income			
Finance Income			
Charge per Session	**£8.00**	**Finance Outgoing**	
Finance Income			
Total Income			
Hydrotherapy	£3529.00	Before Tax Salaries	
Vibro-acoustic Therapy	£112.00	Hydrotherapy	£458
Rebound Therapy	£128.00	Vibro-acoustic Therapy	£108
Therapeutic Music	£96.00	Rebound Therapists	£264
Reflexology	£104.00	Therapeutic Music	£166
		Reflexology Salary	£144
Training Income	0000	**Training Costs**	
		Operating Costs	
		Admin Costs	**£80**
		Repairs/Maintenance stock	
		Total Outgoing	

Note: 1 Hydrotherapy ran for 12 months of the year. Other therapies began in March 2015.

Appendix – Investment Plan: Planned Projects and Projects Being Considered for 2015/16

Planned projects for 2015/16

Install an extra hoist in hydrotherapy suite
New trampoline room with overhead hoist and in-floor trampoline
Continued repairs and maintenance of hydrotherapy suite

Projects under consideration for future years

Replacing the floor surface in the hydrotherapy suite and refurbishing the changing rooms and toilet areas

Appendix – Performance management framework

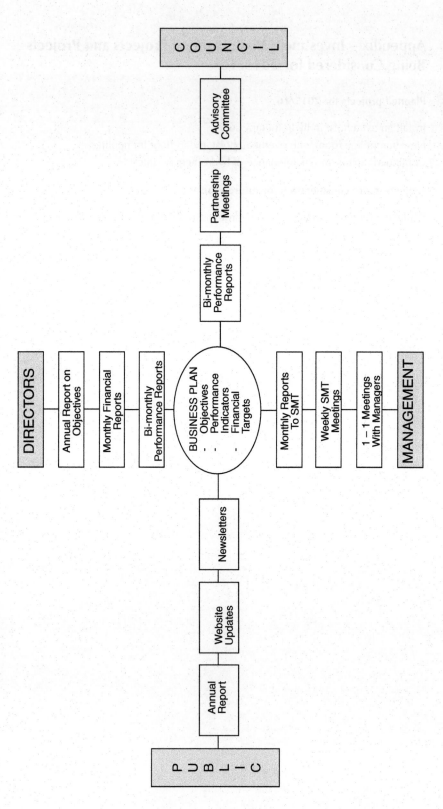

COUNCIL

Advisory Committee

Partnership Meetings

Bi-monthly Performance Reports

DIRECTORS

Annual Report on Objectives

Monthly Financial Reports

Bi-monthly Performance Reports

BUSINESS PLAN
- Objectives
- Performance Indicators
- Financial Targets

Monthly Reports To SMT

Weekly SMT Meetings

1 – 1 Meetings With Managers

MANAGEMENT

Newsletters

Website Updates

Annual Report

PUBLIC

Resource 10.2 Hiring of School Premises Policy and Fee Structure

Table 10.1 Referral and Assessment Form

REFERRAL DETAILS

Date of referral	
Therapy requesting (Please tick)	Hydrotherapy Vibro-acoustic Therapy Therapeutic Music Trampoline Therapy Sherbourne Dance Therapy Reflexology

Person making referral

Name	
Job title	
Employer	
Telephone number	
Email address	

(Continued)

(Continued)

Service user details

Name: Mr/Mrs/Miss/Ms	Forename: Surname:
Date of birth	
Address	
Telephone number	
Email address	
Preferred/first language/Communication Style	

Details of GP

Name of GP	
Surgery address	
GP telephone number	

Responsible person on call (if not main carer)

Name	
Address	
Contact telephone numbers	

Medical information

Please list all relevant medical information for reference only:

Mobility

Levels of Mobility	Yes	No	Other concerns
1 Mobilises independently			
2 Transfers independently			
3 Walks with an aid			
4 Transfers with assistance			
5 Uses a wheelchair			

*Care staff will need to be on hand to mobilise service user during therapy.

(Continued)

(*Continued*)

Communication

Clear and retains information	Yes	No
Some speech impairment	Yes	No
No verbal communication but can indicate needs	Yes	No
Uses sign language	Yes	No
Uses pictures	Yes	No
Unable to indicate needs	Yes	No

Preferred method of communication and other comments:

Co-operation (if 'yes' to 4 and 5 behaviour risk assessment required (FT.04a)

1 Actively co-operates	Yes	No
2 Requires encouragement	Yes	No
3 Co-operates passively	Yes	No
4 Unable/unwilling to co-operate	Yes	No
5 Can display behaviour requiring management	Yes	No

Other comments:

Details of main carer

Name: Mr/Mrs/Miss/Ms	Forename: Surname:
Address	
Telephone numbers: Home Work Mobile	
Email address	
Preferred/first language	
Relationship to person with care needs	

Other professionals' involvement

Name	Contact details
District Nurse	
Occupational Therapist	
Physiotherapist	

(Continued)

(*Continued*)

Name	Contact details
Community Psychiatric Nurse	
Speech Therapist	
Continence Nurse	
Pharmacist	
Other	

Preferred therapy day

Mon	Tues	Weds	Thurs	Fri	Sat	Sun	Occasional

Additional information

Permission to share information we hold on you

To be completed by person with care needs and/or main carer as appropriate.

We are registered with Data Protection. Under the Data Protection Act all information that you have shared with us is confidential.

On occasion we may need to share the personal information you have given us with other professionals involved in supporting you and your carer. These professionals have appropriate exemption under the Data Protection Act which enables them to access personal information. This could include Social Services, your General Practitioner, the Community Nursing Services.

Do you give us permission to share this information?   **Yes/No**

(I acknowledge this with my signature below.)

For the Care Quality Commission (CQC)/Care and Social Services Inspectorate Wales (CSSIW) *(delete as appropriate)* to check the quality of the service we provide, their inspectors may ask for the names and addresses of our clients so that they can seek your views.

I do/do not want the CQC/CSSIW to contact me.

The Commission/Inspectorate *(delete as appropriate)* has the power, under law, to examine your personal file which we hold in our office. We are obliged to allow them to do this.

In line with safeguarding legislation, we are legally bound to report to the appropriate authorities any incidents we observe or become aware of that are classed as abusive as defined in the safeguarding vulnerable adults and children policies and by the Local Authority.

I acknowledge that you have informed me of your legal obligations to the Commission/ Inspectorate *(delete as appropriate)* **and under the safeguarding vulnerable adults and children's policies.**   **Yes/No**

(I acknowledge this with my signature below.)

As part of our training programme and ongoing staff supervision we are required from time to time to observe staff working in the home setting. Also, as part of our induction training for new staff members, it may be necessary on occasion for two care workers to visit your home. This would be by prior arrangement only.

Would you have any objection to this happening?   **Yes/No**

Person with care needs signature:

Carer's signature:

Assessor's signature:

Date:

(Continued)

(Continued)

Table 10.2 Emergency Contact Information

All information will be held in confidence and only used in an emergency.

Name: Address: Telephone No: Mobile No:

IN EMERGENCY PLEASE CONTACT:
 	
 Name:
 	
 Relationship:
 	
 Telephone: Daytime:
 	
                          Evening:
 	
                          Mobile:

MEDICAL INFORMATION: *Please provide us with the following information, which may help us in an emergency to seek appropriate assistance.*   Condition: e.g. Asthma/Diabetes/Angina: Current Medication:
KNOWN ALLERGIES:e.g.: Plasters/Nuts/Penicillin:

Signed:

_____

Review Date . . . .

This policy has been written by the Governors of and runs alongside the hiring procedures set out by the local authority.

There are three levels of charge for the facilities at the school which are:

1 Free lettings – group 1

These are usually for school-related activities, Governing Body events and multi-disciplinary meetings such as Annual Reviews, Social Services, and health professional meetings regarding students of the school and education meetings regarding the students of the school. A free let ensures that the County Council insurance is aware of any such activities. There is no charge made for free lettings; however six weeks' notice is required over the use of the room as the room will be booked and a week's notice if the meeting has been cancelled. These lettings refer to meeting rooms and the dark room (which is used by the Sensory Services) and not the hydrotherapy pool/Soft Play. These will not be a free let.

2 Non-profit-making – schools, local community groups or events – group 2

The charging structure must be fair, transparent and sustainable. It is important to remember that when the school's premises are being hired, the inescapable running costs should be covered in full, therefore cost-neutral solutions should be identified. Although not exhaustive, the key charges may include the following:

- Building Supervision i.e. Caretaking; • Cleaning (cleaning requisites); • Energy; • Accommodation (premises management, maintenance, security); • Equipment (purchase, hire, replacement); • Wear and Tear; and • Administration.

In any arrangement permitting community use of schools, responsibility for the management, control and supervision of the activities being conducted should rest firmly with the user groups. In order to protect the interests of the user groups and the school in respect of public liability claims, it is expected practice for user groups to hold commercial insurance in relation to public liability risks. (Copy of the policy needs to be shown when booking the premises.)

Adequate system of inspection and maintenance in relation to the school premises and grounds and the records pertaining to this will be retained in accordance with the School's Record Retention Policy. Any public liability claims arising from a defect to the school premises will be covered by commercial or self-indemnity arrangements for the school in respect of public liability. These groups are usually from schools, the local community who wish to hold an event for charitable or community purposes or those who need to

(Continued)

(*Continued*)

use the hydrotherapy pool. Such groups may include students from schools in the local authority requiring hydrotherapy, the health service, education committees, church charity events etc. The fee for this type of letting should not leave the school 'out of pocket' and would include energy costs, caretaker time during the event as well as setting up and clearing away. A booking form is required, and a full week notification of cancellation or charges may still be made.

3 Private bookings – group 3

These bookings are from organisations or individuals who wish to hire the premises for events or functions such as parties, private/public meetings, private/public use of hydrotherapy pool/Soft playroom etc. Private/public use of the hydrotherapy pool requires completion of a registration document and must be signed by a physiotherapist. In addition to the fees charged for group 2 events there will also be a scale of charges for different facilities and resources. A booking form is required, and a full week notification of cancellation or charges may still be made.

Additional information

- The bookings are made at the discretion of the school Head teacher who will consider suitability of event, security of the school and availability of required facility given the school's busy timetable.
- Alcohol may not be consumed on the premises.
- The school has limited toilet facilities for adult use during events.
- The school has ramped access at the front and rear of the building.
- Where the caretaker is required to be called out, there is a minimum two-hour booking charge.
- Food technology facilities can only be used with the expressed permission of the Head teacher.

Hire of facilities charging rates

Non-profit-making e.g. schools, local community groups or events
Hire of Pool/Soft Play Weekdays 3.30pm to 7.00pm and weekends 9am–1pm
£ ... per session per person
Hire of rooms during this time to be negotiated in respect of staff and energy costs.
Hire of Pool Weekdays 4.00pm to 7.00 pm and weekends 10am–3pm
Staff Costs £ . . . per hour
Energy Costs £ . . . per hour

Wear & Tear Costs £ . . .

Cleaning Costs £ . . . per hour

Minimum booking is an hour, which includes use of hoist, music, changing facilities etc.

Hire of Pool Weekdays 9.30pm to 3.30pm

Charges will be made like the use of local pools but with the addition of costs for the heating of the pool.

There will be no charge for the use of the pool physiotherapy assistant's and her assistant's time, but this will be reviewed on a yearly basis.

Admission charges:£ . . . per session. Hirer charges are reviewed annually.

Use of Therapy Rooms and Staff Weekdays 4.00pm to 7.00pm and weekends 10.00 am–3.00pm

Staff Costs £ . . . . per hour

Energy Costs £ . . . . per hour

If the rooms are to be hired on a regular basis then a cheaper rate may be agreed. Please speak to the school Finance Administrator to discuss this.

Booking forms below

1   Hydrotherapy pool
2   Trampoline Therapy/Vibro-acoustic room/Music room/Sherborne Dance room

The School – Pool Booking Form

Send to: Finance Office, The School, Address, Tel no.

Date of Hire: Time Required:

Name of Hirer:

Address:

Name of trained pool leader:

Please organise the qualified pool leader before booking the pool – you will be asked for this information when booking.

Costs: Hire Fee _____ hours @ £ _____ per hour

TOTAL HIRING FEE: £

I enclose cash/cheque made out to THE SCHOOL for £

I confirm that I have read the rules for the pool contained in the school Pool Booklet and agree to be bound by them. I have enlisted the help of a lifesaver and agreed to pay for any damage caused by any member of our group. No food will be consumed in the pool area and all rubbish will be taken home with us.

Signed _____ Date_____

(Continued)

(Continued)

The School – Therapy Room Booking Form

Send to: Finance Office, The School, Address, Tel no.

Date of Hire: Time Required:

Name of Hirer:

Address:

Costs: Hire Fee _____ hours @ £ _____ per hour

TOTAL HIRING FEE: £

I enclose cash/cheque made out to THE SCHOOL for £

I confirm that I have read the rules for the Trampoline Therapy room contained in the Therapy Booklet and agree to be bound by them. I agree to pay for any damage caused by any member of our group. No food will be consumed in the room etc. and all rubbish will be taken home with us.

Signed_____ Date _____

Terms and conditions of hire

Hirer

The Hirer must be over 18 years of age and shall be the person by whom the application form for the hiring is signed. Such person shall be responsible for the payment of the fees payable in respect of the hiring and for the observance and performance in all respects of the conditions and stipulations contained in the hire agreement.

Where a prompting organisation is named in the application that organization shall also be considered the Hirer and shall be jointly and severally liable hereunder with the signatory.

Attendance

The Hirer shall ensure that the number of persons using the premises does not exceed that for which the application was made, and approval given.

Fees and charges

Hirer charges are reviewed annually; the current charge is available on booking form at time of hiring.

The hire fee shall be paid in full upon signing the Hire Agreement together with any returnable deposit required by the Board of Governors.

Duration of the hire period

The Board of Governors shall determine in advance the duration of the hire period.

Cancelling of hiring by Board of Governors

The Board of Governors reserves the right to refuse any application. The right is reserved to cancel any hiring, without notice, where the Board of Governors considers it necessary for any cause outside their control. The Board of Governors reserves the right to cancel this Hire Agreement at any time where the Hirer is in breach of the terms of this Agreement and no compensation shall be payable to any person in consequence of cancellation. In such event, the Board of Governors shall not incur any liability to the Hirer other than for the return of any fee or the appropriate part of any fee paid in respect of the hiring.

Cancellation or postponement by Hirer

Hirers will be allowed to cancel or postpone such bookings with a minimum of 24 hours' notice given. Refunds or fees payable will still be charged in the event of less than 24-hour cancellation notice, late notice and non-arrivals.

Hired area

Access is strictly restricted to the hired area and any toilet facilities, entrances, exits and corridors as directed by the Board of Governors. The Board of Governors and Governing Body reserve to themselves, and their officers, the right to enter the hired area at all times on producing evidence of their identity.

Variation of conditions

There shall be no variation to the conditions of hire without the express consent of the Board of Governors.

Care of school premises

The Hirer is responsible for everyone who is on the school's premises for the activities they are organising and, generally, for everyone who comes on to the parts of the school's premises which are under the Hirer's control at the stated times. The Hirer is responsible for ensuring that they comply with all the terms of the hire agreement. No notices or placards shall

(Continued)

(Continued)

be affixed to, lean upon or be suspended from any part of the school premises. No bolts, nails, tacks, screws, pins or other similar objects shall be driven into any of the walls, floors, ceilings, furniture or fittings. The Hirer shall ensure that no persons using the permitted area wear shoes with stiletto heels or other footwear which may in the opinion of the Board of Governors be damaging to the floor surfaces of the hired area. No alterations or additions to any electrical installations either permanent or temporary on the hired premises may be made without the written consent of the Board of Governors. Electrical apparatus must be switched off after use and plugs removed from sockets.

Health, safety and condition of premises

The Hirer/Hirers shall during the hiring be responsible for

(a) Taking all measurers necessary to ensure that the permitted number of persons using the hired premises is not exceeded;

(b) The efficient supervision of the hired premises and for the orderly use thereof including the observance of the Board of Governors' policy on smoking on school premises;

(c) Ensuring that all doors giving egress from the hired premises are kept unfastened and unobstructed and that no obstruction is placed or allowed to remain in any corridor giving access to the hired premises;

(d) Ensuring that all proper safety measures are taken for the protection of the users of the premises and equipment including adequate adult supervision where young people are concerned;

(e) Familiarising themselves and the users of the premises with the fire alarm positions, the locations of the fire fighting equipment and the establishment's exit routes;

(f) Ascertaining the location of the nearest emergency telephone;

(g) the provision of a suitable first aid kit;

(h) The administration of first aid;

The Hirer shall at the end of the hiring be responsible for

(a) Ensuring that the hired premises are vacated promptly and quietly;

(b) Ensuring that the hired premises are left in a safe and secure condition and in a clean and tidy state;

Failure to comply with these conditions may lead to additional charges. The Hirer shall not permit or suffer any damage to be done to the hired premises or any furniture or equipment therein and shall make good to the satisfaction of the Board of Governors and pay for any damage thereof (including accidental damage) caused by any act or neglect by himself, his agents or any person on the hired premises by reason of the use thereof by the Hirer.

Accidents

The Hirer shall immediately inform the Head teacher of the school of any emergency, accident or serious incident that occurs on the school premises. The Hirer will complete and lodge with the school an accident report form.

Intoxicating liquor

Intoxicating liquor shall not be brought into nor consumed on school premises without the prior consent of the Board of Governors. Where such consent is given the Hirer must comply with the Licensing Laws and provide evidence of such to the Board of Governors.

Smoking

There shall be no smoking on the school premises or the school grounds.

Public entertainment and other licenses

The promoters of entertainment and functions to which the public are admitted on payment shall be responsible for completing to the satisfaction of the Board of Governors all formalities in connection with the use of the premises for that purpose. Where the Chief Fire Officer or Licensing Authority require additional premises may be made without the written consent of the Board of Governors. Electrical apparatus must be switched off after use and plugs removed from sockets.

Health, safety and condition of premises

The Hirer/Hirers shall during the hiring be responsible for

(a) Taking all measurers necessary to ensure that the permitted number of persons using the hired premises is not exceeded;
(b) The efficient supervision of the hired premises and for the orderly use thereof including the observance of the Board of Governors' policy on smoking on school premises;
(c) Ensuring that all doors giving egress from the hired premises are kept unfastened and unobstructed and that no obstruction is placed or allowed to remain in any corridor giving access to the hired premises;
(d) Ensuring that all proper safety measures are taken for the protection of the users of the premises and equipment including adequate adult supervision where young people are concerned;

(Continued)

(Continued)

(e) Familiarising themselves and the users of the premises with the fire alarm positions, the locations of the fire fighting equipment and the establishment's exit routes;

(f) Ascertaining the location of the nearest emergency telephone;

(g) the provision of a suitable first aid kit;

(h) The administration of first aid;

The Hirer shall at the end of the hiring be responsible for

(a) Ensuring that the hired premises are vacated promptly and quietly;

(b) Ensuring that the hired premises are left in a safe and secure condition and in a clean and tidy state;

Failure to comply with these conditions may lead to additional charges. The Hirer shall not permit or suffer any damage to be done to the hired premises or any furniture or equipment therein and shall make good to the satisfaction of the Board of Governors and pay for any damage thereof (including accidental damage) caused by any act or neglect by himself, his agents or any person on the hired premises by reason of the use thereof by the Hirer.

Facilities for the purpose of a letting (such as 'Exit' sign and emergency lighting) which are not already installed.

It shall be the responsibility of the Hirer to provide such facilities of an approved type and method of installation. Payment for admission shall be deemed to include admission by tickets or programs or by any other method by which the making of a payment entitles a person to admission. No entertainment or function to which the public are admitted shall be allowed unless the premises are licensed for the purpose under the bylaws of the Local Council in whose area the premises are situated and all necessary regulations against fire are complied with.

The Hirer shall be responsible during the function or entertainment for which the premises are hired for ensuring:

- All safety requirements and recommendations of any licensing authority are complied with;
- any limitation on the number of persons admitted imposed by any licensing authority or the Board of Governors or Governing Body are complied with;
- Suitably qualified persons are employed to be responsible for the supervision of the premises and the conduct of those attending to avoid personal danger, and damage to the premises.

Copyright and performing rights

No copyright work shall be performed without the license of the owner of the copyright and the payment of any appropriate fees.

The Hirer shall comply with all the provisions of the Copyright, Designs and Patents Act 1988. If the Hirer shall fail to do so any permission previously granted by the Board of Governors to use the school premises shall be immediately cancelled and the Board of Governors shall have the right to recover fees, charges or any other payments referred to in this Hire Agreement.

The Hirer shall indemnify the Board of Governors and Governing Body from and against all actions, proceedings, costs, claims or demands whatsoever, arising out of the performance of Copyright Works on school premises.

The Hirer shall, immediately after any performance or function at which music has been performed or songs sung, complete, sign and return to the Performing Right Society a Performing Right Society Limited form obtainable from the Performing Right Society Limited, 29–33 Berners Street, London W1T 3AB.

If it is proposed to play a copyright record or tape in public, application for a license so to do must be made to Phonographic Performance Ltd, Upper James Street, London W1F 59E. Evidence that the necessary licenses have been obtained must be supplied to the school at one week/month* (delete as appropriate) before the letting.

Gaming

No betting, gaming or gambling is allowed except in accordance with the conditions e.g. charitable bazaar, sale of work, fete, dance or sporting event of the Betting, Gaming, Lotteries and Amusement Order 1985 as amended by the Betting and Lotteries Order 1994 when gaming is carried on at an entertainment promoted for raising money to be applied for purposes other than private gain.

Use of Equipment: The hire area does not include the use of any equipment except where specifically agreed and subject to any fees deemed appropriate by the Board of Governors. School furniture (other than chairs for use in halls) shall not be moved except by arrangement.

The Hirer must do everything reasonable to avoid loss, damage or breakage to the school's property whilst the school's premises are under the Hirer's control. Any loss, damage or breakage must be reported as soon as practicable to the Head teacher.

The Board of Governors will be entitled to charge the Hirer for any such loss, damage or breakage on terms to be approved by the school.

Indemnity

The Hirer will be required to indemnify the Board of Governors and the Governing Body against any liability at law in respect of any accident involving death or bodily injury to any person or damage to or loss of any property real or personal and happening consequent upon or in connection with the use of the premises unless due to the negligence/default of the Board of Governors and/or the Governing Body, their servants or agents.

(Continued)

(Continued)

Insurance

The Hirer shall affect and maintain Public Liability Insurance. The level of insurance cover shall be in respect of any one claim and without limit in respect of the number of claims made in any 12-month period of insurance, such insurance to be affected with a reputable insurance company and evidenced immediately upon any reasonable demand.

Parking of vehicles

The parking of vehicles on the school's property shall be permitted in approved areas only on condition that persons bringing such vehicles on to the premises do so at their own risk and that they accept responsibility for any damage to the school's property or injury to any person whether connected with the establishment or not, caused by such vehicles or their presence on the school's premises.

Exclusion of liability

Except in so far as the Unfair Contract Terms Act 1977 (or any statutory modification or re-enactment of it) otherwise requires, the Governing Body will not be responsible or liable in any way whatsoever to any person whatsoever (and whether or not there shall be any negligence by its servants or agents) in respect of:

(a) Any damage or loss of any property brought on to or left upon the hired premises either by the Hirer or by any other person;

(b) any loss or injury which may be incurred by or done by or happen to the Hirer or any person resorting to the third premises by reason of the use thereof by the Hirer;

(c) Any loss to breakdown of machinery, failure of electrical supply, fire, flood or government restriction which may cause the hiring to be interrupted or cancelled;

(d) the Hirer shall be responsible for and shall indemnify the Board of Governors and the Governing Body, its servants and agents against all claims, demands, actions and costs arising from the Hirer's use of the hired premises or from any loss, damage or injury suffered by any person arising in any manner whatsoever out of the use of the hired premises.

Miscellaneous

The Hirer shall comply with such additional conditions as the Board of Governors or Governing Body may require in writing, to be observed for a letting. It is understood and agreed that the Board of Governors and Governing Body do not, either expressly or by implication, warrant the premises to be fit or suitable for any sporting, recreational or other purpose for which the Hirer intends to use them but rely entirely on the skill, knowledge and expertise of the Hirer in choosing so to use them and require the Hirer to discontinue that use immediately upon it becoming reasonably foreseeable that by reason of their condition a participant in or spectator to that sport, recreation or other activity, or any other person is in danger of suffering injury, loss or damage.

General

The Hirer and his agents shall during the hiring and during such other times as they or any of them shall be on the hired premises for the purpose of the hiring comply with all reasonable requirements of the caretaker of the hired premises.

The Hirer shall not sublet the hired premises or any part thereof and in the event of this conditions being breached or any threat thereof then the hiring will stand cancelled, the charges forfeited, and the Hirer and sub-hirer excluded from the hired premises.

Any notice or necessary action required in respect of this hiring may be undertaken by: (a) the Chairman of the Board of Governors or his nominated representative. The right of entry to the hired premises at any time during the hiring is reserved for authorised officers and employees of the Governing Body, the Chairman of the Board of Governors and the Head teacher of the school or a person authorised by them.

Where the hire of the facilities is for a block period this shall be for no more than nine months for any period of hire and shall be reviewed at that time before a decision is made for the hire to continue.

Resource 10.3 Service Level Agreement

After School Provision Club
Leisure, learning and wellbeing
opportunities for adults who have a learning disability

Referral to service

Prior to commencement of any service a referral/assessment form should be completed along with a signed Service Agreement.

Appointments and fees

Each appointment session must be booked in advance as the Therapies do not currently offer a drop-in service. Each therapy currently costs . . . . per session and needs to be paid in full on commencement of the service either by cheque made payable to The School or electronic Bank Transfer, both methods need to reference the name of the person receiving the therapy and the dates of the booking. Unless we are in breach of our terms and conditions all booked sessions must be paid for regardless of attendance.

Cancellations received with less than 24 hours' notice will not be refunded. If cancellations are received with 24 hours an alternative therapy will be offered if available or carried over to the next block of sessions. We reserve the right to cancel a session if late attendance will result in over running another appointment. We will give 2 months' notice of any increase in fees which will be reviewed at the beginning of every year.

Opening times

The service will operate Monday–Thursday evenings 4pm–7pm, Saturday 10–12 noon; this may be subject to change during the School Holidays. All therapies are ½ hour in duration.

Service user/parent/carer/support staff commitment

- Service users need to be on site **10** minutes prior to commencement of treatment.
- Each service user needs to be accompanied appropriately by their parent/carer/support staff.
- Hydrotherapy – service user must be accompanied by a parent/carer/support staff in the pool.
- **Parent/carer/support staff must ensure that they bring suitable clothing to enter the pool.**
- Trampoline Therapy – service user must be accompanied on the trampoline. **Parent/carer/support staff need to ensure that they bring suitable clothing for the trampoline.**
- Service users always remain the responsibility of parent/carer/support staff.

Please bring your own towel, sling (if necessary) and suitable clothing for hydrotherapy. Please bring towel or Kylie pad for Vibro-Acoustic Therapy if necessary. Service users can also bring their own cushion or pillow and their choice of music if they would prefer. Drinking water is available for those who require a drink after a therapy activity.

Manual handling

Individuals who use the school for leisure activities are being supported to attend by members of their families or their support staff. The manager of the person's living situation is responsible for the manual handling plan/risk assessment. Individuals need to take their bespoke slings for all transfers. Two competent persons, who have been trained in safe manual handling techniques, must carry out all transfers. The individual may be supported by the member of their familiar support staff team and assisted by a member of staff, trained in manual handling, from the therapy staff. The exception to this is hydrotherapy where the individual will require the support from two of his/her regular support staff team. All risk assessments will remain the responsibility of the person in position of manager, who has arranged for the individual to attend the sessions. A copy is required to be held by the therapy service manager. It will remain the responsibility of the author to ensure continuity and to evaluate on a regular basis. These guidelines will be reviewed on an annual basis.

Contraindications

It is the responsibility of the service user/parent/carer/support staff to ensure that they have read and understand the contraindications for the chosen therapy service and that they agree to obtain GP consent to ensure no adverse reactions to any treatments.

Termination of sessions

One month's notice is required by either party for termination of agreement. If service users choose to leave prior to the end of their notice, fees are non-refundable. We reserve the right to terminate the Agreement with immediate effect in case of non-payment of fees, or if a service user/parent/carer/support staff displays abusive, threatening or otherwise inappropriate behaviour, or for any other reasonable cause. Intimidation or abuse of our staff will not be tolerated and may result in immediate termination. In all other cases the standard termination period of one month will apply.

Insurance

The service has extensive insurance cover provided by the school. Details of insurance may be requested from The School directly.

(Continued)

(*Continued*)

Personal property and belongings

The service cannot be held responsible for any loss or damage to any service user/parent/carer/support staff property or belongings. Every reasonable effort will be made by the service staff to ensure that property and belongings are kept safe and not damaged.

Accidents and illness

We reserve the right to administer first aid and emergency treatment if required. Parent/carer/support staff will be informed of all accidents and will be asked to sign an accident form. If emergency treatment at hospital is required, then the service would expect the service user's parent/carer/support staff to accompany them and authorise any necessary emergency treatment.

We may require a service user to withdraw from the service if they suffer an illness or medical procedure which has contra-indications for any of the therapies in the service. We may also withdraw service if we have reasonable cause to believe that the service user is suffering from or has suffered from any communicable disease or infection and there remains a danger to other service users who may contract it.

Agreement

These terms and conditions represent the entire agreement and understanding between service users/parent/carer/support staff and the service.

Any other understandings, agreements, warranties, conditions, terms and representations, whether verbal or written, expressed or implied are excluded to the fullest extent permitted by law. We reserve the right to update/amend these Terms and Conditions at any time. One month's notice will be given of any changes made.

The service is run as a partnership project between . . . . and The School.

I have fully read and understand these Terms and Conditions and agree to be bound by them.

Signed: _____ **Date:** _____

Print Name: _____

On behalf of Service User: _____

Position: (Service user/parent/carer/support staff/Care Manager/Health Professional)

_____

Trampolining competitions and programmes

The number of people with disabilities involved in sport and physical recreation is steadily increasing around the world. There are Olympic medal winners and high-performing athletes with diagnosed learning disabilities of ADHD and Asperger's as well as a host of other physical disabilities. There are now organized sports for athletes with disabilities divided into three main disability groups;

- Sports for the deaf
- Sports for persons with physical or sensory disabilities
- Sports for persons with intellectual disabilities

Historically those with physical or sensory disabilities were excluded from competing in sport. From the late 1980s, organisations began to include athletes with disabilities in sporting events such as the Olympic Games and Commonwealth Games. British Gymnastics established Disability Gymnastics to develop and provide training and competitions for all disabled people.

Trampolining became an Olympic sport in the year 2000. It is part of the Gymnastics events. It is not yet a Paralympic sport. To become a Paralympian event enough disabled people must compete. In 2012 Baroness Tanni Grey-Thompson[1] said of gymnastics, 'Many disabled people will take part in this sport, but I would imagine that there are not enough at this current moment in time for it to become a Paralympic event'.

If we want trampolining, which is a gymnastic sport, to become a Paralympic event we need to encourage more trampolining competitions both regionally and internationally. I was speaking to a trampoline club official recently who told me that she had lost some potentially good trampolinists to wheelchair basketball. Wheelchair basketball is already a Paralympic sport. The Paralympic Games is now the second-largest sporting event in the world and is the pinnacle of a disabled sporting athlete's career. Find out more at www.paralympic.org

The International Sports Federation for Athletes with Intellectual Disability (INAS-FID) was established in 1986 in the Netherlands by people who wanted to promote the participation of athletes with mental handicaps in international sports. It promotes sport worldwide for athletes with an intellectual disability, autism and Down Syndrome. INAS-FID provides competition opportunities for elite athletes worldwide. The INAS Global Games takes place the year preceding the

Paralympics. Currently Trampolining is not included. Athletes who compete in INAS-FID competitions can also compete in International Paralympic Committee events. Find out more at https://INAS.org

The Deaflympics is the sporting summit for athletes who are deaf, have hearing loss or tinnitus. The Deaflympics are held every four years and sanctioned by the International Olympics Committee. Trampolining is currently not included in the Deaflympics. Find out more at https://Deaflympics.com

The Special Olympics is the world's largest sports organisation for those with intellectual disabilities and physical disabilities. It was founded in 1968 in America. It was recognised by the International Olympics Committee in 1988. The Special Olympics focus on providing year-round training and a programme of regional, national and international competitions throughout each year. Tumbling, which is both a gymnastic and trampoline sport, was included in the 1972 Special Olympics. Find out more at www.specialolympics.org or www.specialolympic-sgb.org.uk

The Trampoline World Championships

The first national 'rebound tumbling' competition was held in America in 1947. The first-ever Trampoline World Championships were held in 1964 in London. Any gymnast who wishes to compete under the British Gymnastics National Grading Structure must be a member of British Gymnastics (BG). This includes Double Mini-Trampoline (DMT) and Tumbling (TUM).

Trampolining for People with Disabilities (TPD) follows the same rules as trampolining, which can be found in the BG Code of Points unless otherwise stated in the BG Competition Handbook. All competitors must have a disability recognised by international disability sport organisations. In order to be eligible for BG National Disabilities competitions, all competitors must have completed and submitted a Disabilities Gymnastics classification certificate. Disabilities definitions are laid down by BG following those definitions recognised by the World Health Organisation. Category 1 = Learning Disability; Category 2 = Physical or Sensory Disability.

The Trampoline Proficiency Award scheme devised by BG is built around 15 award levels, each offering a variety of skill development. Awards 1–5, suitable for pre-school and beginners, are designed to provide an all-round grounding for trampoline as well as being a suitable training programme for people with a disability.

Awards 6–10, suitable for gymnasts from 5 years to 10 years, develop the actions from 1–5 through a set of challenging skill sets. Awards 11–15, suitable for competitive gymnasts aged 11 and above, allow for progression to a competitive standard and incorporate individual skill development, drills and routines.

The routines for Regional and National competitions can be found in the BG Competition Handbook and online at www.bucs.org.uk

The rules for competing in certain categories are very strict and it is the responsibility of clubs to ensure that the rules are understood by the gymnast and/or their parent/guardian. Any gymnast with Down Syndrome must be screened for Atlanto-Axial instability before being allowed to compete. If a competitor competes in a mainstream Regional competition, they are no longer eligible to compete in the Disabilities section. If they are already competing in Regional but wish to move to disabilities (as disabilities was not available to them before) they will need to write to the disabilities committee at British Gymnastics and ask permission.

There are two pathways of performance, the Regional Disabilities Development Plan and the National Disabilities Pathway. There are no qualifying scores to pass from one pathway to another, so it is down to coaches to choose the suitable pathway to support their gymnast.

There are strict rules regarding trampoline costume attire for competitions which must be adhered to. Visit the BG website to find out more about competing in TPD competitions.

The Trampoline and DMT League is a non-profit organisation in the UK, run by volunteers. The league was set up in 2014. It provides extra events parallel to the British Gymnastics NDP competition system. The league gives the opportunity for trampolinists to practice competing and performing their routines to an audience. The league provides disability trampolining events. Disabilities must be recognised by the World Health Organisation as in other competitions already listed. The trampoline league is similar to what trampolinists used to refer to as the league before BG changed the structure of their competitions. Some clubs still prefer to compete in a league-type competition where you can compete at any level and move up the league. There are also cash prizes to be won. To find out more about the trampoline league go to www.trampolineleague.com

Gymnastics for People with Disabilities (GMPD) is an adaptation of mainstream gymnastics covering all disciplines and can be recreational or lead to competitive opportunities.

British Gymnastics has been developing a programme for disabled gymnasts starting with motor activities for those with more severe mobility problems, leading on to a foundation programme for more able gymnasts.

The disability groups can be split into four major categories as follows:

* Learning,
* Physical,
* Hearing and
* Visual Impairments.

Currently a motor activities programme is being developed which will provide a framework through which even the most profoundly disabled gymnast can participate.

There are many competitions that are devised by clubs that have their own framework to suit the needs of their members. The club officials I met have devised appropriate competitions to meet the needs of their members and those of competing clubs. If you run a club then you can get advice on competitions from the BG website or from any of the home nations disability sports organisations websites. I was shown record keeping at some of the clubs I visited, and it seems an important priority to show progress to develop skills and assess in preparation for competition entry.

It is worth noting that I met with club managers and officials who were very proud to have members with Autism (ASD) and Attention Deficit Hyperactive Disorder (ADHD) competing at a national level with the aim of being selected for the GB squad.

After speaking to different officials representing different trampoline clubs, I found that they all seemed to agree that when a club wants to organise its own competition there are priorities. These are:

* Check out public liability insurance of the building you are going to use
* Appropriate equipment and resources are available

- First aid provision is available
- Copies of consent forms and screening forms should be available
- Risk assessment is available
- Entry fees should cover all expenses
- Transport arrangements confirmed
- Coach or committee member wearing a club T-shirt or tracksuit available for support or to act as marshal
- Judge/s confirmed
- DBS checks for those involved
- Volunteers/parent helpers nominated as a point of contact
- Location instructions and competition timetable sent out in advance
- Appropriate kit
- Photo/media permission sought
- Celebration of members' achievements

Types of competitions you may want to hold

- **Closed** competitions – These are by invitation only according to your club rules.
- **Open** competitions – These are offered by clubs both in and out of their region.
- **NDP** competitions – Routines are set by British Gymnastics and cover from low-level club/inter-club competition up to NDP Level 6 leading to qualification to the NDP Team Finals (and individual Semi-Finals) and the NDP Finals. More information on the BG website.
- **Performance and Elite** competitions – The competitors who achieve the qualification scores will qualify to either the NDP Finals (Performance) or to the British Championships. A downloadable PDF is available from its website: https://www.british-gymnastics.org>competitions-handbooks>trampoline
- **Schools/Colleges** competitions – These are open to all school-aged children and are run by BSGA. It has produced 12 pages of comprehensive guidance to support school competitions, including those for students with disabilities. This is downloadable from: https://www.british-gymnastics.org>competitions-handbooks>trampoline
- Rebound Therapy.org provides a framework that schools can use. It is available on the website starting from Grade 1 and 2, which are competitions for those with profound and complex needs, right up to Grade 8 and it uses the Winstrada scheme to devise the format. Rebound Therapy.org also provides examples of certificates, entry forms, competition programmes and score sheets on its website. Go to www.reboundtherapy.org to find out more.

Winstrada is the international body for the promotion and development of recreational and therapeutic gymnastics and trampolining. It provides teaching resources, development schemes, wall charts and check-off sheets as well as badges and certificates. All of these are available free of charge from the website at www.winstrada.com/

Club competition roles

Competitions require volunteers for official roles. A competition cannot go ahead without these volunteers. Clubs that enter competitions provide their officials.

Chair of Judges – Needs to be qualified and preferably experienced in the role. The judge directs the panel of judges when to be ready to judge and directs trampolinists when to commence their routines.

Panel Judges – To become a judge there is a two-day course. You will watch the routines, score them, total the scores and pass these on to the chair. There is a judging guide at https://highflyers.co.ukjudging.htm. Judges can move up from club judges to county judges, then regional judges, Zonal judges, National judges and finally, International judges. Training is required for each level.

Competition Marshal – Organises trampolinists so that they warm up and perform on time.

Computer Recorder – provided with a table of competitors and a column for scores; keys in scores on a laptop.

Manual Recorder – Acts as back-up to the Computer Recorder (in case IT not working).

Note

1 https://www.bbc.co.uk/news/magazine-19477447.

12 | Trampolining and disability sports support

In this chapter I will just deal with those organisations available in the UK as their information and free resources can easily be accessed via the internet. I reference them as a starting point so that you may take advantage of the free support and resources wherever you are. You will need to ensure that they comply with the laws of your own country if you are not in the UK.

The home nations disability sports organisations all provide training and workshops for coaches, leaders, teachers and volunteers reflecting the diversity of need and identifying good practice within the chosen sport. All the organisations are charities and are listed next.

The Activity Alliance is the new name for the English Federation of Disability Sport (**EFDS**) website – www.activityalliance.org.uk
Disability Sport Wales (**DSW**) website – www.disabilitysportwales.com
Disability Sports NI (**DSNI**) website – www.dsni.co.uk
Scottish Disability Sport (**SDS**) website – www.scottishdisabilitysport.com

If you visit their different websites, you will find that the resources available to you include:

- Welfare and safeguarding toolkit (DSW)
- Useful resources related to welfare and safeguarding (DSW)
- Equality standard guidance and resources (DSW)
- Guidance and resources for clubs (DSW)
- Guidance and resources for education staff (DSW)
- Guidance and resources for local authorities (DSW)
- Guidance and resources for health professionals (DSW)
- Sports Coach UK – Specific coaching awareness top tips for ASD, ADHD, Asperger's Syndrome, Dwarf conditions, hearing impairment, learning disability, manual wheelchair, visual impairment (DSNI)
- Sports Coach UK – Coaching Disabled People Information sheet (SDS)
- Sports Coach UK – Disability Coaching Tips Factsheet (SDS)
- Sports Coach UK – Inclusive Coaching Quick Guide (SDS)
- Inclusive Communications Factsheets (EFDS)

- Mencap: Let's Get Active Guide (EFDS)
- Mencap and Special Olympics GB (EFDS)
- Mind-Get Set to Go (EFDS)
- PDF on British blind sporting opportunities (EFDS)
- PDF on sporting opportunities for those with Cerebral Palsy (EFDS)
- PDF and video on Deaf Sport (EFDS)

In addition, the DSW website provides guidance and support on its INSPORT NGB programme. It is a toolkit to support the development of inclusivity across sport and leisure activities. I met with Fiona Reid, the 2019 Chief Executive Officer of Disability Sport Wales, who was passionate about the programme and how it can 'initiate and then support cultural change across the sectors' and how the programme supports 'disabled people to become more active and engaged (either as players, or volunteers, or coaches)'. Information on INSPORT can be found on the DSW website. Fiona told me that 'sports participation rates for people with disabilities are consistently lower than any other population group and DSW were working hard to change that' (pers. comm. June 7, 2019).

Appendix

1 British Gymnastics Association Trampoline Proficiency Award

British gymnastics Trampoline award scheme begins at Badge 1 for beginners and progresses to Badge 15.

1
1 Waiting in turn, show good behaviour round trampoline
2 Mount /dismount to/from central position on trampoline
3 Move or be freely moved around the trampoline
4 Sitting and bouncing/rocking
5 Standing and bouncing/rocking
6 Lying on back being bounced
7 Hands and knees bouncing rocking

2
1 From seat position, using arm movements bounce
2 Hands and knees bouncing
3 Bounce a set number of times and stop
4 Roll in the horizontal position
5 ¼ twist in an upright position
6 Seat landing, not returning to feet
7 Show star position

3
1 Straight jump using arms
2 Tuck jump
3 Astride jumping
4 ½ twist jump
5 Star jump
6 Back bouncing (with assistance)
7 In a set number of bounces show at least 2 skills

4
1 Tuck jump, touching below the knee
2 Straddle jump
3 Seat drop returning to feet
4 Link 2 ½ twist jumps
5 Split jumps
6 Hands and knees to front landing
7 Repeat a skill 3 times without any intermediate bounces

5
1. Five straight jump, stop and stay still for 3 seconds
2. Tuck jump with stretch and touch
3. Straddle jump
4. Front landing onto mat
5. Back landing onto mat
6. Seat drop to feet, ½ twist
7. ½ twist, seat drop, to feet
8. **ROUTINE** – Straddle Jump, seat landing to feet, tucked jump, ½ twist jump, straight jump and stop

6
1. Seat landing, ½ twist to feet
2. Seat landing, ½ to feet, seat landing, to feet
3. ½ twist to seat landing, to feet
4. Full twist jump
5. Front landing, to feet
6. Pike jump
7. Forward roll
8. **ROUTINE** – Straddle jump, seat landing to feet, tuck jump, ½ twist jump, pike jump, seat landing ½ twist to feet, straight jump and stop

7
1. ½ twist to seat landing, ½ twist to feet
2. Seat landing, ½ twist to seat landing, to feet
3. Back landing, to feet
4. Hands and knees forward turnover to back, to feet
5. Seat landing, to hands and knees, to feet
6. Front landing to feet, seat landing to feet
7. Seat landing to feet, front landing to feet
8. **ROUTINE** – Front landing to feet, tuck jump, ½ twist jump, straddle jump, seat landing to feet, pike jump, full twist jump, straight jump and stop

8
1. Seat landing, to front landing, to feet
2. Front landing, to seat landing, to feet
3. Front landing, ½ twist to feet
4. ½ twist to front landing, to feet
5. Back landing, ½ twist to feet
6. ½ twist to back landing
7. Five back bounces
8. **ROUTINE** – Straddle jump, seat landing, ½ twist to feet, pike jump, front landing, to feet, tuck jump, hands and knees, forward turnover to back, to feet

Pass required in 6 out of 7 and routines up to award 10.

9
1. Front landings pike and straight shapes
2. Back landings in pike and straight shapes
3. Front landing to back landing, to feet
4. Back landing, to front landing, to feet
5. ¾ forward turnover from feet, to back landing, to feet
6. Seat landing, full twist to seat landing (Roller)
7. Backward roll

ROUTINE – Full twist jump, straddle jump, seat landing, ½ twist to seat landing, ½ twist to feet, pike jump, back landing, ½ twist to feet, tuck jump, ½ twist jump, straight jump and stop.

10
1. Seat landing, ½ twist to back landing
2. Back landing, ½ twist to back landing (Cradle)
3. Front landing, ½ twist to front landing (Turntable), to Feet
4. Hands and knees forward turnover to seat to feet
5. Front landing or back landing full twist to feet
6. Full twist to back or front landing
7. Back landing, back pullover to feet
8. Front or back somersault

ROUTINE (A) Full twist jump, straddle jump, seat landing, ½ twist to seat, ½ twist to feet, pike jump, back landing, ½ twist to feet, tuck jump, front somersault (Tucked)

OR

ROUTINE (B) Back Somersault (Tucked) seat landing, half twist to seat, half twist to feet, pike jump, back landing, half twist to feet, tuck Jump, full twist jump

11
1. Front somersault piked
2. Shaped jump, front somersault piked, ½ twist ×3
3. Back somersault tucked
4. Back somersault tucked, tuck jump ×5
5. Back somersault tucked, seat landing
6. Back somersault straight or piked
7. Back somersault straight or piked, straddle jump
8. ¾ front somersault to back, ½ twist jump to feet, shaped jump ×3
9. ¾ front somersault to back, to front landing

ROUTINE – A three somersault routine using somersault to back, to front landing

12
1. Barani straight legs
2. Barani straight legs, ½ twist jump, straddle jump ×3
3. Barani to seat landing
4. Back somersault straight or piked
5. Back somersault straight or piked, shaped jump ×5
6. ¾ front somersault straight
7. ¾ front somersault straight, ½ twist to feet, shaped jump ×3
8. Back somersault tucked to seat, ½ twist to feet
9. Back somersault tucked, back landing
10. Back somersault tucked, front somersault piked
11. **ROUTINE –** A four somersault routine with no somersault link

146

13
1 Barani tucked
2 Barani piked
3 Back somersault tucked, barani tucked
4 Back somersault piked, barani piked
5 Back somersault, barani, shaped jump ×3
6 Back somersault straight, ½ twist jump, shaped jump ×3
7 Back somersault tucked to back landing
8 ¾ front somersault straight, bounce roll, ½ twist to feet
9 ¾ back somersault straight, through straight to back landing
10 Barani, jump to back landing
11 **ROUTINE –** A six somersault routine, including a back somersault to barani link

14
1 Barani straight
2 Back somersault straight, back somersault tucked
3 Barani piked, back somersault piked
4 Back somersault, barani, repeat in different shapes
5 1¼ front somersault tucked to front landing, to feet
6 ¾ front somersault, ball out tucked, ½ twist jump
7 Back somersault straight, piked or tucked with early ½ twist
8 ¾ back somersault straight with early twist, ½ twist jump
9 Full twisting front somersault
10 Front somersault piked, front somersault tucked
11 **ROUTINE –** A seven somersault routine which can be used in competition

15
1 ¾ front somersault straight, barani ball out tucked
2 Back somersault tucked, three quarter front somersault straight, barani ball out piked
3 Full twisting back somersault
4 Back somersault, barani, full twisting back somersault, tuck jump
5 Rudi
6 One and ¾ front somersault tucked
7 Back somersault straight, back somersault piked, back somersault tucked ×2
8 ¾ back somersault, cody tucked
9 Back somersault tucked, ¾ back somersault straight, cody tucked
10 Back somersault straight, barani straight, back somersault piked, back somersault tucked, barani tucked ×2
11 **ROUTINE –** A ten somersault routine with no repeated somersaults

2 Total Communication Policy

Definitions

Co-ordinator   the staff member at the school who has been given lead responsibility to promote good communication practice in the school

Pupil(s)   a child (or children) who undertake their education at the school

SaLT   Speech and Language Therapy

SaLT   Team Speech and Language Therapy service provided by NHS

SMT   School senior management team

Governor   the governor nominated with the responsibility for SLC within the school

Total Communication 'an approach that seeks to create a supportive means of communication to understand and be understood' (Royal College of Speech and Language Therapists)

Ethos

The School is committed to Total Communication, an approach which aims to ensure that people with communication difficulties should have appropriate, coherent and consistent support to meet their communication needs so they can make themselves understood and understand others to the best of their ability.

This policy is the result of collaboration between School staff and the SaLT Team. It will be reviewed in accordance with the School's cycle of policy review, or as deemed necessary by the School's SMT. Any such review will endeavour to take account of research that is relevant to the application of Total Communication within the context of the School.

What is communication?

Communication is fundamental to teaching and learning. It is a two-way process through which information, ideas, thoughts and feelings are passed between individuals and/or groups of people.

Communication is central to life, human rights, inclusion and all areas of human development.

The development of communication skills for all learners at School is an integral part of the curriculum and should not be seen in isolation from other learning goals.

Total Communication requires attention to the methods of communication that are relevant to the individuals concerned.

In adhering to the principles of Total Communication the School aims to:

- provide opportunities for learners to develop a meaningful and functional system of Total Communication using verbal and/or nonverbal communication,
- ensure that all learners feel included with their preferred method of communication which facilitates the opportunity to be understood, responded to and to make decisions,

- integrate fully our approach to communication within all aspects of the curriculum, about literacy and its elements of speaking and listening and
- enable access to the curriculum through a Total Communication approach.

This may include:

- speech and spoken language, including English, Welsh and/or other languages relevant to children in the School,
- non-verbal communication, e.g.: facial expression, eye pointing, gestures, vocalisation, body language such as gestures, body language, intensive interaction,
- use of visual support, e.g.: symbol-based communication such as PECs, schedules, now/next boards, pictures,
- signing, e.g.: The School uses Makaton as a constant multi-modal form of communication,
- objects of reference, including signifiers,
- on body signing,
- communication passports, transport passports, stop and talk prompts,
- assistive technology, e.g.: switches, Eye Gaze, Big Macs, iPad, individual communication aids
- social stories.

Teaching and learning styles – ensuring a total communication environment

Communication is an integrated part of every lesson and curriculum area throughout every day. Teaching and learning take place in a variety of settings, including educational visits, snack and lunch times, play activities, and activities in therapeutic or enrichment settings.

Communication skills can be developed through individual, paired, group or whole class activities. Pupils will be encouraged to communicate with each other through working collaboratively, and sharing their work and experiences, as appropriate. This communication may be verbal, using signs, symbols, objects of reference or electronic communication aids.

All staff use non-verbal communication, such as symbols, signing, body language and gesture, to aid pupil understanding.

Appropriate levels of speech are always observed.

The School uses Communicate in Print for symbols and to support written materials as appropriate.

The School has an agreed set of symbols which are used as markers to identify key areas of the School.

Each classroom has a visual timetable on display. Children may have an individual timetable, using appropriate symbols, according to their support needs.

The most appropriate symbol according to the needs of the individual learner is used, rather than dictating one specific system. This allows for flexibility and responds to the individual need of the learner.

The School uses Makaton signing to support verbal communication throughout the school day, including but not limited to lessons, assemblies, Sing & Sign Choir etc. On body signing is used as appropriate to the needs of the children.

Symbols and communication aids are also used as part of displays in corridors and class-rooms.

The School incorporates specific strategies into learning experiences to maximise all pupils' engagement and ability to develop their communication skills, e.g.: intensive interaction, sensory stories, PECs, TACPAC, POPAT, Story Massage, Objects of Reference.

The School will also use appropriate written materials, e.g.: worksheets, signs, posters, to ensure that children are exposed to writing as a fundamental element of the school setting, reflecting its ubiquity in their wider environment.

The use of 'Objects of Reference' is recognised as an intrinsic part of our approach to Total Communication. Each class is provided with a set of objects relating to the principle activities in school, so that consistency of use is achieved for the children to develop their understanding of routines and activities.

Ensuring a Total Communication environment also entails enabling children in the School to communicate using a method or methods that is most appropriate for them, e.g.: Eye Gaze equipment empowers those who need it to be able to communicate.

The School uses green observation folders to record SaLT activities in 1 to 1 situation and/or pair and group work. The SaLT team works with class teachers to include children's targets in their class lessons as well as into their IEP targets.

Classes run Social Communication groups as part of their morning sessions. Teachers place children into Social Communication groups according to their social skills assessment and run sessions on a chosen morning each week.

The Welsh learning context

The Welsh frameworks for Literacy, Numeracy and Digital Competency set out the skills in these areas that learners may be expected to acquire during their time in statutory education, and which must be delivered across the whole curriculum.

Routes for Learning is an assessment tool developed in Wales to support those working with learners, including children, who have profound and multiple learning difficulties. It provides guidance on communication and cognition developmental pathways.

Teachers at the School must use these documents to plan appropriate learning opportunities throughout the school day so that children at School can learn, practice and develop their communication skills across the full range of learning and social contexts.

School improvement planning

Communication is a priority within the School Improvement Plan in order to promote pupils' wellbeing and to maintain and further improve teaching.

Speech and language therapy

The School values the professional knowledge and input that pupils receive from the SaLT Team and regards them as a critical partner in meeting pupils' communication needs.

The School will ensure that a programme of support set up for a pupil by the SaLT Team will be delivered in School time for the pupil concerned. Where it is not feasible to deliver such a programme the School will contact the SaLT Team promptly to enable the programme to be reviewed.

Where school identifies the need for a SaLT referral the School will follow the standard procedure set out by the SaLT service.

If necessary, the School may adapt resources provided by the SaLT Team to meet the needs of specific pupils.

The SaLT Team will be invited to send a representative to the annual review of each pupil in School who has a SaLT programme provided by the SaLT Team.

Where a pupil receives private SaLT, the School will endeavour to work with the private SaLT provider as if they were a member of the SaLT Team.

Assessment, recording and reporting

The SaLT Team will make an initial assessment of a learner on request. This may involve individual work with the learner, consultation with class staff, learner observation and parental liaison. Ongoing assessment is then facilitated by class staff as part of their agreed curriculum monitoring, including the use of Individual Education Plans (IEPs).

All IEPs should be pupil accessible, with pupil-friendly targets on display in each classroom. These pupil-friendly targets should be referred to during teaching and learning throughout the school day.

A formal SaLT report is provided for each learner's annual review of their statement of Special Educational Need, and an annual written report is produced by the School at the end of the educational year. Parents and carers also can discuss their child's progress at termly parents' evenings. Both the School and the SaLT Team are happy to provide reports at times other than these for specific purposes e.g.: reassessment.

It may at times be necessary for SaLT and the Communication Co-ordinator to observe pupils within their class/group in order to assess and provide constructive support and advice.

Working with parents and carers

The School is committed to working in partnership with pupils' parents and carers in the development of their child's communication, e.g.: facilitating joint meetings with the SaLT Team, providing advice and resources for use at home.

The School has an 'open door' policy and welcomes parents' and carers' input with all aspects of their child's care and education while at School, including their communication needs.

The School will provide training events to support parents' and carers' communication knowledge and skills, e.g.: Makaton training, Parent Partnership.

Parents complete a communication placemat for their child as well as a communication questionnaire when their child starts school and/or new children arriving throughout the year.

Teachers work with parents to complete transport placemats and stop and talk cards to help support children's communication in and out of school.

Professional support

The School will identify a named staff member who has responsibility to lead on developing communication capacity within the School.

The School will ensure that all School staff have access to training in communication every year. The nature and content of such training will be determined by the SMT, taking account of the recommendations of the Co-ordinator, e.g.: Makaton, PECs, Elklan as well in line with the School's School Improvement Plan. Staff can request communication training for their continued professional development via their appraisals and professional developments.

Communication training will also be made available to other members staff, e.g.: midday supervisors, transport escorts etc.

An audit of communication training provided in School is kept and monitored by our CPD coordinator.

Induction

Communication training is provided to all new staff following our school's induction procedure.

New staff and/or long-term supply are taken through our Total Communication presentation which makes explicit reference to expectations relating to supporting speech, language and communication. Every class has a keeping safe book, including communication placemats and the Total Communication Policy which new staff and supply staff are to read and sign.

Supply staff are made aware of Total Communication via our School's leaflet and our online training via the School website.

Equal opportunities

All learners are entitled to appropriate support and intervention relating to the development of their communication, regardless of their race, culture, gender, disability and socio-economic background.

3 Niemann Pick C disease

Niemann Pick C disease is a degenerative genetic disorder. Harmful quantities of fatty substances, called lipids, accumulate in the spleen, liver, lungs, bone marrow and brain. There is currently no known cure for Niemann Pick C disease. Please go to npuk.org to find out more.

4 Meltdown

A meltdown is when a student with ASD experiences cognitive overload or adverse reactions to sensory input more frequently than ordinary mainstream pupils. As a result, students with ASD have a greater tendency to move from a calm and alert state (PNS) to a fight or flight state (SNS) in the presence of certain sensory stimuli. This is known as 'having a meltdown'. Our students may perceive sensory input that seems normal to mainstream students as overwhelming or even painful. This explains why they often experience a fight or flight in the presence of these sensory stimuli. Each student with autism is unique and so is very different in terms of the type or amount of sensory input that causes this reaction. They can have a hard time with self-regulation and actually need assistance to calm. It is important to find what triggered the reaction. When they are experiencing fight or flight, they may attempt to escape the situation or hide, they may become aggressive, or they may cry/scream inconsolably or may even shut down or fall asleep. Every human being reacts differently to situations – that's what makes us individuals. We need to remember that responding from a behavioural point of view is ineffective in these cases. As adults, we need to remove the excessive or adverse stimuli, and we may need to take the student to a calm, quiet place.

- Some students may need to be held.
- Some may need to exercise to get excess energy out and decompress.
- Others may prefer to sit alone with a comfort blanket that feels weighty (proprioceptive input also known as deep pressure input) so that they feel grounded.
- Some may like the visual stimuli of low lighting.
- Others may prefer auditory stimuli of music.
- The smell of essential oils works for some.
- Water play works for others.
- Others may prefer to sit with something to twiddle as a tactile stimulus.
- Certain types of vestibular sensory input (sometimes referred to as movement input) can also help: Some of our students who are in the midst of a sensory meltdown respond positively to swinging on a swing or rocking in a chair, while other children prefer to jump on our outdoor trampoline in times of stress.

It is important to have a basic understanding of sensory input that can calm individual students (as each child has an individual response to sensory input). Individuals with autism have meltdowns for various reasons. Autism, after all, is a spectrum disorder. Attempting to reason with a student during a meltdown (sensory overload) is ineffective.

But how do you know when it's a meltdown or when a student is simply having a temper tantrum?

Well, for all intents and purposes, a meltdown does look very similar to a tantrum. Often, it's difficult to tell the difference, especially to the untrained eye or for someone who might not be familiar with autism.

With a tantrum, a student is looking for a reaction whereas with a meltdown, the student does not care if you are reacting or watching. They have simply reached a point when they are out of control and they are very frightened.

This is taken from my slightly longer article on the topic; refer to www.linkedin.com/pulse/having-meltdown-ange-anderson/

5 TEACCH® Policy for Schools

This policy explains the nature of the TEACCH® Approach within the School and its contribution to the education of students at our School.

This policy has been shared and approved by the teaching staff and school governors.

Ethos

Our school is committed to providing access for all students with an Autism Spectrum Disorder (ASD) with access to high-quality services and supporting them in being able to participate in a wide range of everyday and leisure activities as other students in our School do. Our School believes that students with an ASD and their families should have access to effective support from the School and staff should have the necessary knowledge and skills to work effectively with all students with an ASD.

Objectives

In order to value and respect our students with ASD, our School's main objectives for the TEACCH® Approach are:

- To recognise and seek to maximise every student with ASD's potential through using the TEACCH® Approach.
- To raise awareness and develop confidence in the knowledge of students with ASD.
- To ensure that the TEACCH® Approach is supported by developing a shared knowledge, skills and attitudes base essential for part of an effective wider ASD provision environment.
- To ensure we provide students with the most useful and suitable TEACCH® Approach strategies by remaining at the forefront of TEACCH® Approach developments.
- To acknowledge the need to work collaboratively with students with ASD and their families related to the TEACCH® Approach.

The TEACCH® Approach at our School should be a personal and pleasurable experience, which enriches the lives of the students with ASD and those around them.

Rationale

The students with ASD are supported by staff at our School who have specific training in aspects of autism. In addition, staff have received an induction training programme in supporting students with ASD so awareness is spread across the School. Structure, visual support and individualised strategies appropriate for each individual are provided to aid a student with ASD gain access to the curriculum.

What is the TEACCH® Approach?

Within this rationale the TEACCH® Approach 'structured TEACCH®' methodology is recognised as a valuable support to some students with ASD at our School in allowing them to access learning.

The history

TEACCH stands for the **T**reatment and **E**ducation of **A**utistic and related **C**ommunication handicapped **CH**ildren. It was developed in the early 1970s by its founder Eric Schopler, at the University of North Carolina. The TEACCH® Autism Program (TEACCH® Approach) developed the concept of the *Culture of Autism* as a way of thinking about the characteristic patterns of thinking and behaviour seen in individuals with ASD.

The TEACCH® Autism Program (TEACCH® Approach) developed the intervention approach called *Structured TEACCH*, which is based on understanding the learning characteristics of individuals with autism and the use of visual supports to promote meaning and independence.

Principles of Structured TEACCH

- Understanding the culture of autism.
- Developing an individualised person- and family-centred plan for each individual, rather than using a standard curriculum.
- Structuring the physical environment (Independent Workstations, Individual and Play Skills Area).
- Using visual supports to make the sequence of daily activities predictable and understandable.
- Using visual supports to make individual tasks understandable.

The long-term goal of the TEACCH® Autism Program (TEACCH® Approach) is for the student with autism to fit as well as possible into our society as an adult. We achieve this goal by respecting the differences that the autism creates within each student and working within his or her culture to teach the skills needed to function within our society. We work to expand the skills and understanding of the students, while we also adapt environments to their special needs and limitations.

In the same way, educational services for students with autism should have two goals:

1   Increase their understanding.
2   Make the environment more comprehensible.

The TEACCH® Autism Program (TEACCH® Approach) in practice

1   Physical Environment (Structuring the Environment)

A TEACCH® Approach classroom may include the following areas to support students with an Autism Spectrum Condition.

- Play Skills/Play Area
- Independent Work Area
- Daily 1:1 Instruction
- Snack/Lunch
- Structured Play
- Daily Schedule

2   Schedules (Structuring the Day)

A TEACCH® Approach classroom may include the following strategies to support students with an Autism Spectrum Condition.

- First/Then or Now/Next
- Work then some leisure activity or food
- Schedules may be: part day or whole day
- Timeline/schedules can be presented left to right or top to bottom
- Timeline schedules can range from the use of objects to written words
- Visual information should be presented in a neutral transition area

Schedules may be presented as:

- Objects of Reference
- Photographs
- Pictures/Line drawings
- Symbols
- Written words
- iPads
- Combinations of the above

3   Work Task (Structuring the Work)

A TEACCH® Approach classroom may include the following strategies to support students with an Autism Spectrum Condition.

- Work tasks/systems are individualised methods of working and can be used in a variety of contexts.
- They are structured in such a way that helps to understand the following:

  - What work do I have to do?
  - How do I do the work?
  - When am I finished?
  - What am I doing next?

4   Individual (Structuring the Individual)

A TEACCH® Approach classroom may include the following strategies to support students with an Autism Spectrum Condition.

- Individual Schedule
- Individual Work Station
- No displays in the workstation – minimises distractions
- Work from left to right – work 'to do' on the left in tray and work 'finished' should be put to the right
- Activity should be appropriate, and with minimal adult input to maximise independence
- Adults should sit slightly behind or to the left side and use hand on hand if required to guide
- A 'I am working for' reward i.e. photo of favourite activity or item should be visible in the workstation to motivate

Entitlement

We endorse the aims of the National Curriculum to provide a broad and balanced curriculum and deliver the TEACCH® Approach to enable some students with ASD students to access the curriculum.

Implementation

Nursery

- Nursery has a TEACCH® Approach independent workstation.
- Nursery uses a visual timetable and Objects of Reference for the whole class.
- It is the responsibility of the class teacher and HLTA to decide which of the four structured TEACCH® strategies are suitable to be introduced with students with ASD and discussing this with their parents. This is likely to follow discussion with the lead teacher in ASD and SMT members.

Foundation Phase and Key Stage Two

- Students with ASD are mixed into every class for a more inclusive approach.
- It is the responsibility of the class teachers and their class team to decide which of the four structured TEACCH® strategies are suitable to be used with students with ASD and discussing this with their parents. This is likely to follow discussion with the lead teacher in ASD and SMT members.
- Every class has at least one TEACCH® approach workstation.
- Every class uses a visual class schedule displayed on its circle time display board and uses a visual class schedule on its interactive whiteboard.

Whole school

- The active use of TEACCH® Approach strategies will be indicated on the Student with Autism Spectrum Conditions Individual Education Plan (IEP).
- All classes include a whole class daily schedule in the form of an interactive whiteboard transient PowerPoint, communication in print symbols board, Objects of Reference and/or musical cues.
- All classes include individual schedules in the form of iPads, now & next boards, Objects of Reference, transition boards and/or choice activity boards.
- Most classes use sand timers, timed timer and online interactive whiteboard timers to support student with ASD.
- Most classes have a rewards display and use motivators and reinforcers to support students with ASD.
- All TEACCH® Approach resources used to support students with ASD (schedules, symbols, motivators etc) should be transferred with the student with Autism Spectrum Conditions (ASD) to the next class.
- Information regarding TEACCH® Approach strategies used to support students with ASD may be passed on to the next class teacher in the form of a 'TEACCH® Approach Summary document

Training

At our School, there is a commitment to training *all teaching staff* and to give awareness raising training to all teaching assistants in the knowledge and understanding of the TEACCH® Approach when working with students with ASD. TEACCH® Approach training is available to all staff members at our School in the following way:

- Induction – Basic Autism Awareness Training
- Three-day TEACCH® training course available for staff for their continued professional development if requested
- In-house TEACCH® Approach training as part of our ASD Rolling Programme

- ASD Provision Drop-ins for practical help and advice
- ASD online training plan by the Geneva Centre for Autism via School website

Resources

The lead teacher in ASD leads the development of a central bank of resources needed for TEACCH® Approach strategies that class teachers may access, via the School's website, staff common, as well as materials needed in classes.

Equal opportunities

The TEACCH® Approach is delivered to students with ASD regardless of gender, culture or ability. Boys and girls have equal access to this approach.

Monitoring and evaluation of the TEACCH® Approach

The Headteacher carries out detailed monitoring and evaluation of the Nursey and Foundation Phase and the Key Stage Two departments, which includes the delivery of the TEACCH® Approach within these departments. Monitoring and evaluation is carried out on a rolling programme every two years. As part of this programme the ASD Co-ordinator may be asked by the Headteacher to carry out a detailed monitoring and evaluation of the TEACCH® Approach. As part of this process the ASD Co-ordinator looks at all aspects of how the TEACCH® Approach is delivered in school and its relationship to student progress. An action plan for further development is then drawn up.

Supervision

The ASD Co-ordinator and class teacher have overall responsibility for the supervision of all those receiving the TEACCH® Approach. The class teacher will evaluate students with ASD suitability to access the delivery of the TEACCH® Approach and may request the advice of the ASD Co-ordinator and/or SMT members for support.

6 Whole School Approach to DIR® Floortime™

Registration/choice/DIR® Floortime™/regulation/ observations

As the children come into the classroom, they are encouraged to put away their belongings independently. Once their things are organised onto their pegs, they may go to the classes play area/s.

Home school diaries

Every child has a home school diary. Teachers include comments telling parents about their child's experiences including emotions, opinions and reflections. They will be encouraged, if possible, to write and draw about their experiences including emotions, opinions and reflections.

Community learning

Children will participate in activities in the community such as going to the post office, shops, cafe, parks etc. Teachers will notify parents prior to any offsite activities and parents will be required to sign a permission slip.

Self-help

As independence and having a strong sense of self are a strong focus of our whole school approach, self-help targets will be set for each child in termly IEPs and then worked on daily in their morning workgroups.

Morning Circle time/self-esteem/self-expression

Greetings, peer awareness and interaction, music, emotions, abstract thinking (building bridges, sequencing, predicting), Theory-of-Mind, specific social and language skills, attention and independence are all targeted during circle time. The principles of DIR® are incorporated into every aspect of Morning Circle. These activities are alternated with the more instructional portions of circle to keep the children focused.

Snack time

Snack time is the perfect opportunity to build circles of interaction between staff and children. Language and socialisation are both targeted during this highly motivating time. Children are encouraged to ask their friends to share or trade snacks. Commenting and joking are facilitated during this time.

DIR® Floortime™: play skills/peer play/regulation games

This is the time for individual DIR® Floortime™ sessions. This takes place in our 'Playing and Being with Others' activities and experiences sessions. Floortime™ is a philosophy developed by Dr. Greenspan and Dr. Wieder. This approach allows staff to interact with the child at their level, while teaching through meaningful interactions. The basis of DIR® is to help children achieve regulation through relationships while providing them with the foundations needed for all learning. These foundations include the ability to sustain attention to activities and interactions, engage in interactions through a range of emotions, develop adaptive and coping strategies, be initiators of independent ideas and have the ability to sequence these ideas in meaningful ways, develop a good sense of self and the ability to string together ideas and social interactions to problem solve, to think and play symbolically and understand emotions, to use creativity and imagination, to think abstractly, reason and problem solve. Individual, specific language, social, behavioural and academic goals are layered upon these foundations. All goals are targeted through motivating, experience-based interactions with staff and children. Children are placed into the appropriate FEDLS (Functional Emotional Development Levels) based on their Individual Education Plans (IEP), classroom assessments, and staff observations. Observation notes are taken on all skills and monitored closely by the classroom staff present during the sessions. Children are moved through the levels based on the observation notes and their ability to generalise skills to all environments. Additionally, transition skills are worked on to support children transitioning to less restrictive environments. For example, if a child is having trouble raising their hand in circle time in their mainstream inclusion classroom, that skill will be taught and reinforced on an individual basis to make the mainstream experience more successful.

Semi-structured play/peer play/play skills

Specific play and social skills are taught as part of our VIP (Venturing into Play) and Incredible Years curriculum programmes. Introductory skills include finding hidden objects, peek-a-boo games, and physical games such as chase, symbolic play and turn-taking. More advanced skills include imaginary play, sustained interactions and group games. Skills are taught in the same areas the children use them. Staff take on the role of the child and play at their developmental level modelling specific skills. Activities are based on the children's natural motivations and incorporate familiar themes. For example, children use dolls to act out riding home on the bus and familiar afternoon and evening activities. Once children become more independent in their play, staff facilitate sustained peer play and are eventually faded out completely.

IEPs

IEPs (Individual Education Plans) are set for each child and may also be targeted using a variety of approaches including DIR® Floortime™ (experience-based learning), breaking concepts down into smaller steps and the use of visuals. Teachers incorporate activities that target the different levels and learning styles of the children.

Group Floortime™/social skills group: (social theme, peer turn-taking, shared timing, emotions, Theory-of-Mind, abstract thinking, problem solving)

Peer awareness and interaction, abstract thinking (building bridges, sequencing, predicting), problem solving, emotions, Theory-of-Mind, specific social and language skills, attention and independence are all targeted during this time. These skills follow a hierarchy based on our curriculum and the individual needs of the children. Each skill is extensively covered using books, videos, role-play, puppet and doll shows and experience-based activities. After being targeted through a structured lesson, children are encouraged to generalise the skills outside of the circle. Facilitation of these skills followed by verbal reinforcement assist this process. Group Floortime™ and Social Skills Group may take place during class time, incredible years, speech and language and/or as part of our Playing and Being with Others afternoon curriculum.

Abstract thinking/sequencing/problem solving

This section is a large focus of our entire program and also reflects the Greenspan/Wieder philosophy. Our main goal is to help the students become independent thinkers. If they are able to think on their feet, they can do anything. Often children engage in inappropriate behaviours, lack social and language skills, or may seem self-absorbed due to a poor understanding of the world around them. These deficits are targeted through critical thinking activities. The ability to think abstractly, sequence and problem solve are crucial to being an independent thinker and understanding the world. Activities to target these skills include sequencing events using visuals and toys, understanding cause and effect through thought-provoking activities, problem solving and story analysis through role-play, social stories and games. All activities reflect themes familiar to the students. Abstract thinking, sequencing and problem solving are targeted throughout the day incidentally. Recognition of these skills and skill-specific reinforcement is given regularly.

Note: If a child is not able to benefit from this group lesson, they are removed to receive one-on-one Floortime™ with a therapist and reintroduced to the group when ready.

Emotions

Because we believe all learning is emotionally based, this area of instruction is a priority. Instruction includes extensive lessons on specific emotions. Teaching the students to recognise and respond to emotions in self and others through experience-based learning promotes independent generalisation of skills. Enabling the students to acquire a good understanding of their own emotions, and encouraging awareness of peer's emotions, leads to recognising the motivations behind others' emotions (Theory-of-Mind).

Sensory breaks

Children should be warned of the activity five minutes prior to tidy up and getting together. The goal of this activity is to get the blood flowing, provide breaks for the senses and bring body and mind together. Most of the children we work with have particular difficulty coordinating their minds and bodies. Exercise, stretching, yoga, rhythm and timing activities, Brain Gym activities may be used during this time. No matter what the activity is, music as part of the activity is recommended. Different types of music can encourage different types of regulation.

Meditation and mindfulness

During this time, mats are laid out for the students to lie down as relaxing music is played in the background. Students are encouraged to focus on breathing and participate in using visual imagery (closing eyes and picturing a scenario the teacher describes in a calm, soothing voice). A child's form of yoga often follows to help students release built-up tension or anxiety, which enables them to become refreshed and renewed.

Technology

Many of the children in our School benefit from the use of technology in both learning and interacting. This may include some or all of the following:

- iPads (PECs App)
- Computer with Adaptive Technology
- Interactive whiteboard
- Augmentative Communication Device
- Eye Gaze
- Auditory Integration Training
- Neurofeedback
- Virtual Reality

Supported typing/PECs App/Clicker 6/Eye Gaze/ Makaton groups

Facilitated communication is one form of augmentative and alternative communication (AAC) that has been an effective means of expression for some individuals. It entails learning to communicate by typing on a keyboard or pointing at letters, images or other symbols to represent messages. Facilitated communication involves a combination of physical and emotional support to an individual who has difficulties with speech and with intentional pointing (e.g. unassisted typing). Individual sessions support children to communicate through these tools.

There is more information on my LinkedIn article at www.linkedin.com/pulse/floortime-therapy-play-intensive-interaction-ange-anderson/

7 Stimming

Stimming is a shortened term for self-stimulatory behaviour. Students with autism can sometimes be seen hand flapping, spinning, jumping using a fidget toy or using repeated questions, words or phrases. In the distant past these behaviours were frowned upon and discouraged. Nowadays fidget toys are big business and are popular everywhere. It is realised that a fidget toy can help concentration and focus the mind. A fidget toy is a little like a safety valve helping to reduce the pressure of the situation. Virtual assistants such as Alexa, Siri and Cortana can aid students with autism who get into the spiral of continuous questioning.

8 Doman Delacato Patterning Therapy

This therapy involves a series of bodily exercises and activities that move the body in specific patterns that purport to provide feedback to the damaged brain. Find out more at www.iahp.org

Bibliography

Aalizadeh, B. 2016. Effect of a trampoline exercise on the anthropometric measures and motor performance of adolescent students. *International Journal of Preventative Medicine*. Available online at www.ncbi.nimnih.gov>pmc

Anderson, A. 2019. *Virtual Reality, Augmented Reality and Artificial Intelligence in Special Education*. Routledge.

Anderson, A. et al. 2015. *The Future of Special Schools and Therapeutic Intervention*. Available online at www.amazon.co.uk/dp/B01BB7D4VM/ref=cm_sw_em_r_mt_dp_U_AQ.zDbBAW4SHT

Aragao, F.A., Arampatzis, A., Karamananidis, K., and Vaz, M.A. 2011. Mini-trampoline exercise related to mechanisms of dynamic stability improves the ability to regain balance in elderly. Available online at www.ncbi.nih.gov>pub

Baron-Cohen, S. 2004. The cognitive neuroscience of autism. *Journal of Neurology, Neurosurgery & Psychiatry* 75: 945–948. Available online at www.jnnp.bmj.com>content

BBC. 2018. Trampoline parks: Regulation calls after injuries increase. *BBC News*. Available online at www.bbc.co.uk/news/uk

Bedford, R., Pickles, A., and Lord, C. 2015. Early gross motor skills predict the subsequent development of language in children with autism spectrum disorder. *Journal of Autism Research* 9(9): 993–1001, published by Wiley Periodicals for International Society for Autism Research.

Bhattacharya, A., McCutcheon, E. P., Shavartz, E., and Greenleaf, J. E. 1980. Body acceleration distribution and O2 uptake in humans during running and jumping. *The Journal of Applied Physiology* 49(5): 881–887.

Blume, H. 1998, September 30. Neurodiversity. *The Atlantic Monthly*. Available online at www.theatlantic.com

Brancaccio, N. 2014. Available online at https://windsorstar.com/news/autistic-gymnast-aims-for-the-sky

Buchegger, J. et al. 1991. Does trampolining and anaerobic physical fitness affect sleep. Available online at https://journals.sagepub.com/doi/10.2466/pms.1991.73.1.243

Children and Families Act. 2014. London, HMSO. Available online at www.legislation.gov.uk

Cornfield Magazine. 2019, July. Central Birmingham, Solihull & Warwickshire edition by Cornfield Magazine: 18–19. Available online at www.issuu.com>docs>bham_jul

Crocetti, D., Marko, M.K., and Mostofsky, S.H. 2015. Behavioural and neural basis of anomalous motor learning in children with autism. *Brain* 138: 784–797, Oxford University Press. Available online at www.ncbi.nim.nih.gov>pub

Crowther et al. 2007. Kinematic responses to pylometric exercises conducted on compliant and non-compliant surfaces. *Journal of Strength and Conditioning Research* 21(2): 460–465. Available online at www.journals.lww.com

CSP. 2016. Safe practice in rebound therapy. *The Chartered Society of Physiotherapy*. Available online at www.csp.org.uk

Delacato, C. 1963. *The Diagnosis and Treatment of Speech and Reading Problems*. Available online at https://openlibrary.org/books/OL5880629M/The_diagnosis_and_treatment_of_speech_and_reading_problems

Disability Sport Wales. 2019. Information. Available online at www.disabilitysportwales.com/guidance-and-resources-for-clubs/read-the-aims-for-each-insport-club-standard/

Donald, E. 2017, May 30. Local 9-yr-old with autism heads to national gymnastics competition. 07:00 AM, Updated 10:57 PM. *BND Belleville News Democrat*. Available online at www.bnd.com>education

Egge, R. 2013. Trampolines helping people with autism reach new heights. Available online at www.komonews.com>archive>trampolines

Emerson, E. 2009. Estimating future numbers of adults with profound and multiple learning disabilities in England. CeDR research report. *Tizard Learning Disability Review* 14(4) Emerald Insight. Available online at www.emeraldinsight.com

Erlacher, D., Schredl, M., and Blischke, K. 2016. Effects of learning trampolining on REM sleep parameters: A replication study. Available online at Erlacher, Schredl, Blischke Poster NASPSPA 2009 SchlafTramp.

Giagazoglou, P., Kokaridas, D., Sidiropoulou, M. et al. 2013, September. Effects of a trampoline exercise intervention on motor performance and balance ability of children with intellectual disabilities. *Research in Developmental Disabilities* 34(9): 2701–2707. Available online at www.researchgate.net>2390

Giagazoglou, P., Sidiropoulou, M., Mitsiou, M., Arabatzi, F., and Kellis, E. 2015. Can balance trampoline training promote motor coordination and balance performance in children with developmental coordination disorder? Available online at www.sciencedirect.com/journal/research-in-developmental-disabilities

Gillberg, C., and Kadesjo, B. 2003. Why bother about Cumsiness? The implications of having Developmental Coordination Disorder (DCD). *Journal of Neural Plasticity*, published by Hindawi Publishing Corporation.

Gov.UK. 2016. Obesity and Weight management. Available online at www.gov.uk.publications

Hahn, J., Lee, W., and Shin, S. 2015. The effect of modified trampoline training on balance, gait, and falls efficacy of stroke patients. *Journal of Physical Therapy Science*. Available online at www.ncbi.nlm.nih.gov/pmc/articles/PMC4681903/

Heitkamp et al. 2001. Gain in strength and muscular balance after balance training. *International Journal of Sports Medicine* 22(4): 285–290. Available online at www.researchgate.net>1192

Henderson, D. 1999. Special schools should be abolished. *SEN Magazine*. Available online at www.tes.com>news>special

Hippocrates 400BC. On Injuries to the head (translated by Francis Adams). Available online at www.classics.mit.edu/Hippocrates/headinjur/html

Horne, D. Trampolining (a complete handbook). ISBN 0571048684. Available online at www.amazon.co.uk>trampolining

IATP. 2019. Response to CBS news story on trampoline parks. Available online at www.indoortrampolineparks.org/newsroom/IATP, www.skylinetrampoline.co.uk/rebound-therapy/IATP

Internet Encyclopedia of Philosophy. George Santayana (1863–1952). Available online at https://www.iep.utm.edu/santayan/

Jarvis, J. 2019. London Youngsters encouraged to take to trampolines in fight against obesity problem. Available online at www.standard.co.uk>news

Kato. 2004. *Significance of Musico-Kinetic Therapy for Patients with Traumatic Brain Injury*. Available online at www.link.springer.com

Leary, M., and Hill, D. 1996. Moving on: Autism and movement disturbance. *Mental Retardation* 34: 39–53. Available online at www.researchgate.net>1438

MelloMontiero, C.B. de, Crocetta, T.B., de Menezes, L.D.C., de Silva, T.D., Magalhaes, F.H., Massatti, T., and de Moraes, I.A.P. 2017, July–September. Motor learning characterization in people with autism spectrum disorder. *Dement Neuropsychologia* 11(3): 276–286. Available online at www.ncbi.nim.nih.gov>pmc

Noda, R, Maeda, Y., and Yoshina, A. 2004. Therapeutic time window for musicokinetic therapy in a persistent vegetative state after severe brain damage. Available online at www.ncbi.nlm.nih.gov/pmc/articles/PMC4894746

OXSRAD. 2019. Available online at www.msn.com/en-gb/news/uknews/prince-harry-visits-oxsrad-sports-centre-in-oxford/vi-AABm7aW

Rainforth, B., and York-Barr, J. 1996. Chapter 3 in educating children with multiple disabilities by Orelove & Sobesy. Brookes Publishing Co., Baltimore. ISBN: 9780933716735. Available online at www.amazon.co.uk/Educating-Children-Multiple-Disabilities-Transdisciplinary/dp/

Reinders, H.S. 2008. *Receiving the Gift of Friendship: Profound Disability: Theological Anthropology and Ethics*. Eerdmanns. ISBN 0802862322. Available online at Amazon.

Singer, J. 1998. *Odd People in: The Birth of Community Amongst People on the Autistic Spectrum: A Personal Exploration of a New Social Movement Based on Neurological Diversity*. Sidney: Faculty of Humanities and Social Science University of Technology, Sydney, Australia. Available online at www.geniuswithin.co.uk>blog

Singhal, P. 2018. Available online at www.smh.comau.education

Spdstar.org. 2019. The rebounders. Available online at www.spdstar.org

Vuillerme, N. et al. 2001. The effect of expertise in gymnastics on posture control. *Neuroscience Letters* 303(2): 83–86. Available online at www.researchgate.net>1202

Warnock, M., Norwich, B., and Terzi, L. 2010. *Special Educational Needs: A New Look*. London: Bloomsbury. Available online at www.bloomsbury.com

Winter, H. 2002. *Telegraph*. Available online at www.telegraph.co.uk/sport/football/teams/england/3027882/Beckham-bounces-back-to-fitness.html

Zeliadt, N. 2016. Words say little about cognitive abilities in autism. Available online at www.spectrumnews.org>news

Index